IN-LINE SKATING

IN-LINE SKATING

THE ULTIMATE HOW-TO GUIDE

Albert Fried-Cassorla

PRIMA PUBLISHING

P ™ and PRIMA PUBLISHING are trademarks of Prima Communications, Inc.

Photography by Mark Bullard

Library of Congress Cataloging-in-Publication Data

Fried-Cassorla, Albert, 1949-
    In-line skating: the ultimate how-to guide/by Albert Fried Cassorla.
       p. cm.
    Includes index.
    ISBN 1-55958-648-6
    1. In-line skating. I. Title.
    GV859.73.F75 1994
    796.2'1—dc20   94-40280
                                              CIP

95 96 97 98 99 AA 10 9 8 7 6 5 4 3 2 1
Printed in the United States of America

How to Order:

Single copies may be ordered from Prima Publishing, P.O. Box 1260BK, Rocklin, CA 95677; telephone (916) 632-4400. Quantity discounts are also available. On your letterhead, include information concerning the intended use of the books and the number of books you wish to purchase.

This book is dedicated to my wife, Martha,
and to my twin children, Emma and Benjamin Fried-Cassorla.
You guys keep me rollin'!

CONTENTS

ACKNOWLEDGMENTS

Many people have been wonderfully helpful to me in the research and preparation of this book. I would like to thank:

Walt Sherin of Sports 'n Stuff

Tina Radowicz of The Hockey Stop

Berri Goldfarb of the National In-Line Hockey Association

Jennifer Goldstein of Bladin' Action

Zak Hoffstein, who gave special help in the hockey chapter

Dr. Tony Verde of Graduate Hospital's Sports Medicine Center, who was extremely generous with his time and expertise in assisting with my chapters on fitness and racing

Wendy Kelly and Doug Kelly of Landskaters Club

Natalie Kurylco of *InLine Magazine*

Bob Goldwitzer of Delaware Valley In-Line Skating Association

Dwayne Vonfraenkel

Derek Parra

Nick Perna

Henry Zuver of the International In-Line Skating Association

Valerie Zuver, codirector of the Atlanta-to-Athens Road Skating Marathon

Maureen O'Neill and Jennifer Schwegman of Rollerblade, Inc.

Andy Seeleye of USAC/RS

Jill Schulz

Ari Rosenthal

Mark Bullard of Axiom Photo & Design

Scott Cramer

Tod Cohen

Scott Wilhite of the National Museum of Roller Skating

Chris Mitchell and Tad Hofstadler of Wilburger's Ski Shops

Michael Shafran of In-Line Retailer

Jon Bogert and John Horan of Sporting Goods Intelligence

Robert Roth and Bryan Houser of Cheap Skates

Beth Taubman and Cindy Taubman of Fried-Cassorla
   Communications, who helped me proofread and
   edit my manuscript
Benjamin Fried-Cassorla, my son, who helped with
   many tasks

. . . and the many other skaters who helped make this
   a more useful book!

—Albert Fried-Cassorla

The author and his family enjoy a skate along Philadelphia's Kelly Drive, near the beautiful Schuylkill River.

WARNING:

1

AN INTRODUCTION TO IN-LINE SKATING

Welcome to in-line skating, one of the world's fastest-growing sports. Whether you're a beginning or experienced skater, you've come to a sport that is fun, keeps you fit, and gets you places!

This chapter will give you a quick overview of the sport to prepare you for what's coming up in later chapters.

YOU'VE DISCOVERED A SUPERB WAY TO GET FIT AND STAY THAT WAY

If you want to develop muscle tone, burn off calories and fat, and become physically fit, then you can find no better way than in-line skating.

Want to burn off the fat? In-line skating does it beautifully! Expect to burn between 500 and 900 calories per hour. A pound of body fat contains 3,500 calories. If you skate one hour a day and eat at a normal rate for your body, you will lose a pound a week or more.

Here's another reward—you'll increase your rate of metabolism. That keeps fat burning even while you're *not* exercising.

An added benefit: Psychologically, you'll feel more fit. That's because you'll have more reason to eat with your health in mind. You'll come to see yourself as a fit person who's on the way to a more slender body—a shape you'll want to keep. So, naturally, you'll lay off the chocolate cake, cheddar cheese, or whatever your special "fat Jones" is.

A personal note: before I took up in-line skating, I bent the scales at 182 pounds. Now I'm down to 167, skating regularly—and still trying to lay off potato chips.

Not Just Getting Fit but Also Staying That Way

In-line skating not only helps you lose weight and build muscle tone, but also helps you remain in good shape.

Skating feels great, either alone or with a friend!

Lots of people lose weight—but few keep it off. This fact keeps the diet industry thriving. If you don't yet have a favorite activity for staying in shape, in-line skating will be perfect for you. That's because (I confidently predict) you'll enjoy it and will keep wanting to do it.

So many fitness programs fail simply because participants resent the activity! Exercise shouldn't be something you hate but do anyway because it's "good for you." Exercise should be something you *love* to do. There are so many unused stationary bicycles in the living rooms and dens of America because, for many people, bicycling indoors, staying in the same place, is just plain boring. So good intentions dissipate, and idleness results. Love a sport and you'll lose the fat.

If you build in-line skating into your way of life, you'll find that you look forward to your regular outings. And you'll skate more often.

CROSS TRAINING

For some people, in-line skating is a great change-of-pace activity—something that builds strength or endurance and can be enjoyed between other sports. You can cross train for fun or as part of a deliberate plan to excel at another sport. In-line skating can help build key muscle groups for certain highly related activities. Some sports where in-line skating works synergistically to increase strength and endurance include:

- Ice hockey
- Jogging
- Running and sprinting
- Bicycling
- Skiing
- Swimming
- Walking

We cover cross training in greater detail in Chapter 9. For now, keep in mind that even if you're impassioned about another sport, skating can be a valuable alternative activity.

SO MANY WAYS TO HAVE FUN

In-line skating offers many pleasures. In fact, the appeal of pure fun is the greatest reason people come to it. The pleasure motive outstrips all others, including exercise, racing, playing in-line hockey, and cross training.

For most people, in-line skating is a social sport. People are much more likely to skate in groups than to skate solo. And, of course, in-line hockey is a group activity—and it's hockey players who are swelling the ranks of in-liners at the greatest rate. This social dimension of in-line skating means that you'll make friends or cement older friendships, perhaps improving the entire quality of your life.

GLOSSARY

ABEC. An acronym standing for Annular Bearing Engineering Council. ABEC ratings correlate to the speed of the bearing. Lower ABEC ratings mean that a bearing turns at a slower speed.

aggressive skating. Skating with an attitude, usually involving daring moves, including grinds, rail slides, wall rides, and airs, among others.

bail. To fall; sometimes to purposely fall in order to avoid gaining speed and taking an even worse fall.

black ice. Smoothly paved asphalt street.

carve. To skate well, especially on a curved surface.

cheese grater asphalt. Bumpy road.

coping. The upper edge of a ramp, where vertical surface meets a horizontal hanging. The coping is a metal or PVC pipe running along that edge, on which tricks are done.

duck walk. A way beginning skaters acquire balance; walking on skates with feet in a V-shaped position.

durometer. A measure of the hardness of polyurethane wheels. The higher the durometer, the harder the wheel.

freestyle. A type of skate dancing that includes showy moves, usually—but not always—done to music.

half-pipe. A U-shaped ramp used by skaters for various moves.

poser. Someone who likes to wear fancy clothing and use sophisticated equipment, but who doesn't skate.

pylon. A cone used to mark the perimeter of a racing track.

quad skates. Traditional roller skates, with four wheels—two front, two back, side by side.

quarter-pipe. A curved ramp that is flat at the bottom and curves until it rises straight upward.

slam tan. Tan lines produced by knee and wrist guards.

spacer. One of several pieces of the interior of a skate, used to separate the bearings and provide a lining for the axle.

streetstyle skating. A type of skating that is heavy on airs, grinds, and other moves.

torque. Power exerted in a curved motion, as in accelerating while making a turn.

transition. The curved section of a ramp between the flat horizontal and vertical surfaces.

vert. The part of the riding surface of a quarter-pipe or half-pipe that rises straight upward. Vert also refers to skating on ramps, especially in moves involving aerial work.

V-walk. Same as duck walk—a way of learning how to get your balance by walking on skates with your feet pointed outward in a V-shaped position.

Think about all of the ways you can have a blast on skates—it'll increase your appreciation of the sport and might lead you to try something new. You'll enjoy yourself by:

- Being outside during fine weather
- Taking in the beautiful passing landscape, seascape, and sky
- Relaxing with your family and friends, in an activity you can enjoy *together*
- Feeling the sensation of your body moving over varied terrain, the sun on your back, and the wind washing your body
- Growing in agility and skill as you become increasingly comfortable on skates

Make In-Lining a Part of Your Everyday Life

Skating has become a part of everyday life for people all over the United States and around the world.

Even people you'd *never believe* would skate are rolling now! Take the Amish people of Pennsylvania, for example. They're also known as the "Plain People." This group of religious, fundamental Christians rejects many features of modern life, including mopeds and cars. But in-line skates are just fine, they say!

In such Pennsylvania towns as Intercourse and Bird-in-Hand, you will occasionally see men in overalls and straw hats pumping away on in-lines down a country lane. Young women use them, too, especially as a mode of

Rolling—a recipe for romance!

transportation to and from work away from the farm. As reported in the *Philadelphia Inquirer*, an Amish man said of his fellow people, "They get around with them a lot. Instead of hitching the horse up, you just hop on your Rollerblades."

Middle-aged and older people are also enjoying the sport. After all, you can skate at your own pace—taking time whenever you like to slow down and sniff the roses. Moreover, skating spares you the wear and tear on the knees and other joints that may accompany jogging.

SAFETY FIRST

In-line skating is only as safe as your attitude. More people get injured by what they *don't consider* than by what they do.

To skate safely: First, have a safety-minded perspective. Don't attempt more than you're reasonably sure you can handle. Second, buy and wear all of the key protective gear. That means quality skates, an ANSI-, Snell-, or ASTM-approved helmet, and special protectors for your knees, elbows, and wrists. Taking those precautions will help keep you sound, safe, and ready to enjoy the sport!

I devote considerable attention in this book to safety issues, and I urge you to carefully read Chapters 3 and 4: "Getting Started: How to Choose Your Equipment" and "Skating Safer."

Parents can play a big part in reducing their children's chances of an accident. When it comes to critical safety issues, parents shouldn't take "no" for an answer (I don't, from my own kids). See "A Word to Parents" on page 36.

A FEW WORDS ON EQUIPMENT

Make a decision early in your exploration of the sport to get quality skates and protective gear. The expenditure isn't much compared to some sports. About $250 to $500 will get you well under way.

Begin by reading Chapter 3, "Getting Started." Then commit yourself to buying quality gear, with the assistance of a knowledgeable salesperson or friend. If you have high-quality equipment you'll be rewarded with easier skating, better health, and even more fun!

Skate on!

National Museum of Roller Skating

2

A HISTORY OF
SKATING

*T*he history of skating really begins with the invention of that most essential and wonderful of devices—the wheel—which first rolled into the world about 5,000 years ago. Human history would have been very different without this circular tool. Think of it: The wheel made horse-drawn transportation easier and made machinery using cogs (notched wheels) possible. So not just transportation, but entire industries and more efficient agriculture have also depended upon the wheel.

A wheel is actually a form of lever that controls the flow of power. The middle part of the wheel—its axle—corresponds to the fulcrum we know in other levers. We can think of a wheel as a series of levers. At any one moment, one radius is the "force arm" where an initial force is placed and amplified. The other, directly opposite, radius is the "load arm," moving an object.

Historians believe that the wheel was first devised by ancient Mesopotamians in the city of Ur, between the years 4000 and 3000 B.C.E. No, Fred Flintstone does *not* get credit for the wheel! But the first wheels had a passing resemblance to the logs that run beneath Fred's car. These early wheels evolved from logs used as rollers in moving heavy sled loads. Disks cut from logs were attached to the ends of rollers. In India and Java, such devices remain in use today.

What is the oldest wheeled vehicle? It's probably an Egyptian chariot built circa 2000 B.C.E. The wheels it used are not unlike some modern wheels. The Egyptian wheel had a hub, portions of rims called *fellies*, and spokes. Egyptians also developed a wheel with a leather tire that was kept in place with strips of rawhide.

Now our whirlwind history of this sport briefly leaves the wheel behind, as we leap ahead one millennium. That's because roller skating also traces its roots to a *non-wheeled* sport, ice skating. Ice skating deserves equal, if not primary, credit as a source of modern wheel-borne in-line skating.

THOSE SKATING SCANDINAVIANS

Around the year 1100 B.C.E., skating would have been an efficient way to cross a frozen lake in northern countries such as Holland and Norway. Skates might also have been used to help hunters in getting closer to game. Early skates were made of bone attached to leather boot soles. They probably wobbled, but surely they worked!

Whether skating was done solely for work or for pleasure is unclear. Did people two thousand years ago actually have *fun* skating? To my mind, at least, the answer is obvious. How can a person *not* have some fun ice skating?

THE RENAISSANCE AND BEYOND

Skates worked even better once they were made of iron, which was first used in skates in the 1500s. Iron skates offered greater structural stability and strength—people could skate harder in them, and iron was less likely than bone to fracture.

Scotland, a nation of lakes, was the logical and actual center of skating innovation, which blossomed in the 1700s. Edinburgh was the site of the very first skating club. The book you are reading is only the latest in a long history of skating books written to help participants in the sport since that time.

The 1700s also saw the development of the first true roller skates. Credit goes to a Belgian named Joseph Merlin, who—as far as we know—invented the first roller skate. He loved ice skating, but couldn't enjoy it in the summer. In this case, pleasure, rather than necessity, was the mother of invention.

Merlin was a man of many talents, similar in some respects to our own Benjamin Franklin. Like Franklin, Merlin invented musical instruments. Also like Franklin, he invented a diverting gadget, the roller skate. These novelties became part of an exhibit of his inventions that traveled around London.

Though Merlin may have been a magician of sorts, he had no abracadabra for the challenge of stopping while on skates. He crashed often—and badly. Once, during a major public demonstration of roller skating conducted in a ballroom, he collided with a large mirror. His inelegant display led to a hiatus in roller sports for three decades.

The first documented in-line skate was developed and patented in France in 1819 by M. Petitbled. In 1823 Robert John Tylers, a Briton, secured five wheels to the bottom of a shoe, thereby inventing his "Volito" skate. Skating on "skeelers," as they were called, became very popular in Holland. Ice skating was extremely popular there, and wheels were the perfect antidote for the Netherlanders' summertime blues.

But difficulty in turning and stopping still limited the sport's appeal. Tylers even attempted using hooks to form a braking mechanism. Try to imagine "hooking" onto dirt

Illustration of "rinking" from a Winslow Skate advertisement.

and cobblestone roads—just the thought is comical. Tylers did help the art of turning by inventing what we today call "rockering." This is the use of center wheels that are lower (closer to the ground) than the toe or heel wheels. This curve in the line of the wheels eases turning.

Even rockering was not a total answer to the difficulties of skating. Remember that iron skates of those days were crude and difficult to master, especially by today's standards. Stability was hard to come by.

Plimpton and the Four-Wheeled Skate

Enter the four-wheeled skate. An American named James Plimpton invented it in 1863. Now any cowgirl or fräulein could boot up and roll away with a reasonable chance of not crashing. In Germany, fräuleins on skates did, in fact, serve beer to thirsty men, who enjoyed viewing the careening maidens between quaffs.

James Plimpton also became one of the great proselytizers of the sport. He organized clubs, demonstrations, and even the first roller rinks. The sport became truly popular.

Whoosh! Someone Must Have Just Invented Ball Bearings

Roller sports and transportation as a whole got a power injection in 1884, with the invention of ball bearings. Added to early in-line skates, they enabled skaters to glide far more easily. Of course, this improvement made a big difference in both the popularity and practicality of the sport.

Perhaps ball bearings seem like another humdrum invention, a bit player in the theatrical pageant of civilization. Think again. Ball bearings help us to overcome *friction*, and friction reduces our ability to move. In fact,

ball bearings are so important that they're almost as significant as the invention of the wheel itself. Their use goes far beyond skates—cars, trucks, trains, and motors of all sorts depend on them.

Skates as we know them are unimaginable without some form of ball bearings. Simply put: Without them, each stride would be followed by very little rolling.

When rolling became easier, skating became a much more attractive activity. Four-wheeled skates were so easy to master that they became the rage. In-line skates were so much harder to use that they were eclipsed for many decades.

Roller skating became popular throughout the United States. It was good clean fun and easier to do competently than ice skating. Going to a rink became the perfect winter activity for housebound people in industrialized countries around the world.

Skateboarding and the New Wheels

The popularity of skateboarding in the 1960s brought renewed vigor to roller skating. The earliest skateboards were fashioned from ripped-apart roller skates. The front and back sets of wheels were attached to wooden boards, and off people went—on steel wheels onto unforgiving cement.

In the 1970s, polyurethane wheels were put on skateboards for the first time. They gripped the road better and made for a smoother ride. Skateboarding became a way of life in places such as Venice, California, and Golden Gate

Park in San Francisco. Along with the skateboarders came the roller skaters. To them, wheeled life was the life. The popularity of wheeled sports set the stage for the event that made modern skating the sport of millions that it is today.

National Museum of Roller Skating

The original modern in-line skate, produced by Chicago Skate Co. (c. 1960).

SCOTT AND BRENNAN OLSON AND THE REBIRTH OF IN-LINE SKATING

Scott Olson was a devoted ice hockey player. He and his brother Brennan felt that their off-season training routine should be more like true ice hockey. One day, Scott was in a sporting goods store, browsing among some old equipment. He saw an old in-line skate. No urethane wheels. Antiquated construction. But still . . .

Soon, Scott and Brennan were working in their basement, burning with enthusiasm over the possibilities for in-line skates. They developed their forerunner of today's skates by adding urethane wheels and a rubber heel brake. With these improvements, skaters gained maneuverability and stopping power. And the sport felt a lot more like ice skating!

That was 1979. By 1981, Scott Olson was purchasing in-line skates from a manufacturer and selling them wherever he could. He called his in-line skates "Rollerblades." After all, the in-line skates formed a kind of blade that was similar in effect to ice-skate blades. Olson worked hard to improve the design of the skates. For example, he bought a patent from Chicago Skates that enabled him to make the wheel assembly work more efficiently.

Three years later, he sold his fledgling company to a Minneapolis businessman named Robert Naegele Jr. Rollerblade Inc. continued to perfect its line of skates. Among many other accomplishments, the company developed the first all-polyurethane boot and wheels with a stronger, lighter core. Nor have we seen the end of the Rollerblade bag of innovations—stay tuned!

Rollerblade Inc. provided the vision and power to help make in-line skating into a booming sport in the 1980s and 1990s. The company sponsored demonstration tours, racing teams, and other kinds of events. It helped support safety campaigns and helped shape major nonprofit organizations devoted to in-line skating. Today, Rollerblade Inc. is the most successful company in the field of in-line sports. It has served the public and its own interests well by helping the sport grow.

Of course, many companies manufacture skates, as shown by the list in Appendix C. Market leaders include Canstar Sports/Bauer, First Team Sports/Ultra Wheels, and Roller Derby.

MODERN IN-LINING

Interest in in-line skating has grown tremendously in recent years. In 1989, the sport claimed 3,065,000 participants. By 1993, the number was four times as high— it had zoomed up to 12,559,000! How many hard-core participants are among the 12 million? The latest figures show 3.2 million frequent skaters, meaning those who roll 25 times or more per year.

If you believe that in-line skating has a lot in common with ice hockey, ice skating, and skateboarding, you're right. These sports are the source of many newly converted in-line skaters.

Women and men have basically the same level of interest in the sport. Men and boys are more likely than women and girls to become roller hockey players. Women and girls get into the sport for recreational and fitness reasons.

Perhaps it comes as no surprise to you that in-line skates make a great holiday gift. In fact, 30 percent of all in-line skates are purchased in December—this despite the fact that in many parts of the country, December is not at all suitable for skating.

Many organizations promote in-line skating. One of the most prominent is the IISA, or International In-Line Skating Association. The group was formed in 1991 to help the sport in many of its dimensions, including recre-

IN-LINE SKATING PARTICIPANTS BY AGE

Age Group	Number of Participants
6–11	4,866,000
12–17	3,240,000
18–24	1,565,000
25–34	1,822,000
35–54	1,001,000
55 +	65,000

Source: *Rollerblade In-Line Skating Facts*, 1993 figures.

ation, competition, and safety. Its headquarters are open to inquiries of all kinds (see Appendix A).

One appealing characteristic of the sport is that it's open to all income groups. The most popular place for in-line skating is the North-Central states (not either of the coasts!). There, 3.9 million skaters zip around on in-line skates, as compared with 2.8 million participants apiece for the Northeast, South, and West.

Children from ages 6 to 11 make up the largest age group of in-line skaters (see chart on previous page).

Perhaps the main reason why in-line skating draws people from diverse backgrounds and age groups is that the sport itself is so varied. There's enough to offer, in fact, to keep an entire camp going. That was the idea behind Camp Rollerblade.

The premiere Camp Rollerblade was and is in Santa Rosa, California. It was organized for Rollerblade in 1990 by freestyle skater Jill Schulz. The camp's four-day sessions are typically held in late July and early August. Each session covers such aspects of skating as basics, advanced moves, ramps, hockey, figures, freestyle, windskating, and skate-to-skiing (in-line slaloming with ski poles).

A few Camp Rollerblades have been offered in other parts of the country. Costs are about $300 per four-day session. The fee covers instruction, breakfast, lunch, some dinners, and professional instruction. Discounts on lodging are available. For more information, call Snoopy's Gallery and Gift Shop at 1-707-546-3385.

National Museum of Roller Skating

Cartoon from a French newspaper (1849).

The Media Love In-Line, Too

Today, in-line skating is visible everywhere—and is especially prominent on TV and in the movies. Team Rollerblade is often featured in news and sports stories in print and on the air. Its members are a group of talented skaters, acknowledged by many to be the best in their respective specialties. They perform stunt and freestyle skating moves. The exciting team can be seen on in the movie *D2: The Mighty Ducks*, as well as on MTV Sports and CNN. Of course, advertisers love to show vivid scenes, and so Team Rollerblade also appears in ads for such corporations as Kellogg's, Mountain Dew, and McDonald's.

THE FUTURE OF SKATING

The future of in-line skating belongs not to the manufacturers, but to the skaters—to you. Skaters invent new tricks and activities, ask for improvements in skate design, and literally roll back the sporting frontier.

Think of what skates do: They make humans themselves into vehicles! Humans are erect bipeds. The fact that we stand up and walk is part of our essential nature. Skates are an extension of our power to walk or run: They simply make it easier.

The history of skates is still being made. What's past, as Shakespeare says, is prologue. Be a part of it, by continuing to explore this great sport.

3

GETTING STARTED: HOW TO CHOOSE YOUR EQUIPMENT

A pair of excellent skates will surprise you! If you've never been on a quality set of in-line skates, you're in for a treat. First, the fit will be snug and supportive. There's very little room for ankle wobble, as in some ice skates. The fit will be more like that of a ski boot.

And the skates roll—*fast*. So be prepared.

HOW MUCH YOU'LL SPEND

Expect to invest $250 to $500 for your skates and a full set of protective gear. That breaks down to $100–$300 for skates and $150–$200 for safety gear. Don't leave the store without buying, in addition to your skates, a helmet, elbow pads, knee pads, and wrist protectors. We'll cover protective gear in detail later in this chapter.

Try to purchase the best pair of skates you can afford. Make sure they're comfortable, snug and supportive, not too tight at the toes, and not too heavy.

WHERE TO BUY

Don't buy your skates at a toy store. They may offer attractive prices, but the equipment is likely to be inferior. Most important to your shopping success is having access to quality equipment. Almost as important is finding a good salesperson, preferably an experienced in-line skater who will help guide you to what you need—equipment you will grow with. You're likely to find this kind of person at a skating equipment store or at a ski shop that also specializes in in-line skates.

Shop at a store where you can try on skates and roll around, preferably on carpet and near a sturdy countertop or railing that you can lean on. The carpet will help cushion you if you fall. And trying on your skates is absolutely imperative, to be sure of a good fit. Of course, rolling on store carpet is hardly like carving the black ice.

But it will at least give you some sense of the feel of the skate and its rolling action.

Don't think you can't fall on a carpeted floor—I witnessed a gentleman with no protective gear almost take a bad spill within seconds of putting on his skates. His fall was stopped only by the quick reflexes of some friends. Wear protective gear, even in the store.

Mail Order—Good if You Truly Know What You Want

Unless you're absolutely certain which make and model fits you best, don't buy skates through the mail. Experienced skaters who know exactly what they're purchasing will sometimes find good deals via the mail. Even though I have made a living in the direct-mail business for much of my life, I still say that in this case beginners should try on the skates before buying them. In fact, trying on lots of skates is probably best.

BUYING SKATES FOR CHILDREN

Children will be able to learn more quickly and will have more fun with high-quality skates. Too many kids these days are skating on junk. They can't enjoy the flexibility and ease of glide that superior skates offer.

Sometimes it's the shopkeeper's fault. According to skate-shop owner Walt Sherin, "I'll never again steer a parent to cheaper skates for kids. A father and son came into my store. The boy asked to see a pair of $100 skates.

Choose in-line equipment for children carefully.

I led him to a less expensive section of the store and said, 'I think your father would want you to look at these.' I was steering him to the $30 skates.

"The father was outraged! 'How *dare* you presume to know what I can afford to spend on my son!' he said. I had assumed that because the child would be outgrowing the skates that a less expensive pair was called for. I haven't made that mistake since!"

Although children eventually outgrow skates as their feet grow, quality skates can last longer than you might think. With today's adjustable boots and soft liners, you can get a pair that's a little large. Buckles can be made tighter and liners thicker until the child's feet grow. Meanwhile, the youngster gets the benefit of true rolling.

Worth noting is that Roces offers a skate made to expand as youngsters' feet grow. Their St. Louis Jr. has a Growth Compensator liner that expands four sizes.

THE BOOT

The boot should be made of two distinct parts: a shell and a liner.

Some shells are made of one-piece molded plastic. Others are made of two pieces, with a hinged upper ankle section. This allows the upper ankle to flex. However, I believe that a rigid shell is best for most people, especially beginners. It offers maximum support for those who are learning. Some quality boots are made of one-piece leather with a glued-on liner. These skates are very

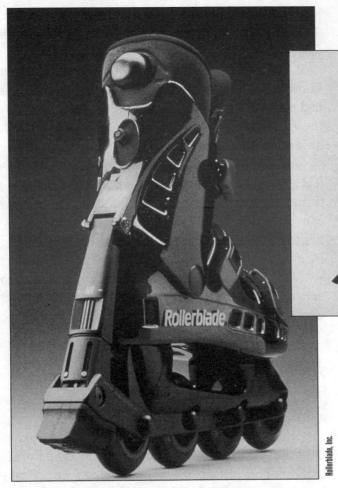

Rollerblade, Inc.

Gaining in popularity are built-in braking mechanisms, such as this type made by Rollerblade, Inc.

Rollerblade, Inc.

popular among racing enthusiasts. For the novice, though, they offer insufficient support and reduced options. Go for a two-piece shell and liner boot with micro-adjustable buckles.

While you're standing in the store in your skates, bend at the knees. Make sure that you can bend, even if it means loosening your upper buckles. Bending is critical to balancing, turning, and stopping.

Shells

The shell should be sturdy, with air holes to allow your foot to breathe. In-line skates are often hot, especially in warm weather. The holes are your air-conditioning.

Shells and one-piece boots are made of various materials. The types of plastics most commonly used are (1) polypropylene, a hard plastic; (2) polyurethane, a softer, rubbery plastic, the same material used in wheels; and (3) polyethylene, a very flexible plastic.

Buckles Are Beautiful!

They're strange things to praise—mere buckles. But good ones make such a difference in ease of use and comfort. They're so much easier to use in getting skates on and off than are old-fashioned laces. And they give you the support you need exactly where you want it.

In an all-buckle boot, expect three micro-adjustable buckles. Look for many tiny ridges along the surface of the buckle strap. Each tiny ridge represents a significant increment of tightness. You need that control over tightness to give yourself support and yet maintain flexibility.

Choosing a Size

When you go to try on skates, wear thin socks. That way, when your skates expand (as they inevitably will), you'll be able to take up the slack by just wearing a thicker sock.

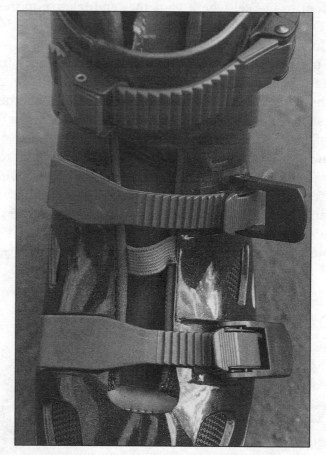

Buckle up!

Before settling on a size, remove the liner and place your foot in it. Feel where your toes end relative to the liner. Do you feel extra room? Not good! Your toes should go right to the end of the liner.

When you put your foot with sock and liner back in the skate, your foot should feel snug, but not tight. Your toes should not hurt from bumping against the end of the skate shell—nor should there be any open space, though you might want that in a regular shoe.

Buckles do have one *disadvantage:* They tend to break from repeated snapping into and out of position. The stress of skating also makes them more susceptible to breaking. Streetstyle and vert skaters pound their skates. If you're passionate about those types of skating, choosing lace-ups may spare you a lot of repair trouble.

High Cuffs

A high shell, one that extends several inches above the ankle, gives a relative rigidity that you'll welcome at first. If you become a true racer, you can always get a low-cut pair of racing skates later in your rolling career. Speed skaters' boots may be constructed of exotic space-age materials to provide extra lightness, strength, and breathing ability, but you're not likely to want them to be your first pair.

Socks for Comfort and Dryness

Though not a part of your boot, your socks play a big part in overall comfort. Get a pair of thin, polypropylene socks. Once you've worn in your skates and created a little slack inside the boot, begin wearing heavier athletic socks over these. The thin socks will wick away sweat into the thicker socks.

Liners

Most skates come with either a joined shell and liner combination or a shell with a removable liner. Removable

A removable liner and its shell.

liners have two advantages. First, they allow you to try different liners and find one that fits you well—provided it's not joined to the shell. Second, if a liner is removable, you can replace it when it gets worn.

Liners are typically made of soft foam sandwiched between layers of nylon. Your liner should help your boot fit your foot in great comfort. In some shops, the salesperson can improve the way your liner and shell work together. For example, people with narrow feet can benefit from pieces of foam added to loose areas. And some liners are made of "memory foam" that conforms to the contours of a person's foot.

Orthotics and Posted Foot Beds

To give your feet more support and reduce fatigue, consider having orthotics or posted foot beds made for your feet. These are contoured materials that mold to the shape of your feet, providing strong support.

You can have orthotics made at a skate or ski shop in about 30 minutes. They are formed by heating a piece of hard plastic until it is relatively soft. This heated plastic is laid atop a bed of foam, called a foot dome. You step with bare feet onto the warm plastic, which molds to your feet. Crouching at this point will simulate actual foot positioning during a skate.

Once it has cooled and hardened, the plastic layer is removed from the foam bed. This layer, which will form your orthotics, is inserted in your skates in place of your insole, the removable bottom part of your skate liners.

For even better support, consider posted foot beds, which are formed by attaching several layers of rubber to the bottom of your orthotics. It takes a little more than an hour to have a foot bed made. The cost can range from about $40 without a purchase, to $135 for a dual-density (extra layered) foot bed.

Orthotics and foot beds can dramatically extend the amount of time during which a person can skate in comfort. If your feet hurt after one hour without orthotics, using these inserts may allow you to go for two hours before fatigue sets in. A worthwhile investment for the serious skater!

FRAMES, CHASSIS, AND RAILS

The frame, chassis, or rail (all different terms for the same item) holds a skate's wheels. It attaches to the boot above and to the wheel bolts or axles below. The frame may be made of nylon, and sometimes fiberglass adds strength. Some frames are made of aluminum. The material used is not as important as the support provided.

Check the frame for strength; a flimsy frame won't give you the support you require. The wheels should be held securely in place. If you're checking out skates in a store, see if you can twist the frame from side to side. In general, the more rigid the frame the better, but a slight amount of give may be no problem.

A feature to look for in the frame's design is provision for adjusting the height of the center wheels. This is useful for rockering, or lowering the center wheels. You want this capability, both in your early days as a skater and when you become more proficient.

WHEELS

Wheels come in various degrees of urethane hardness, known as durometer. Most wheels sold today range from the 70s to the 80s in durometer. The lower the number, the softer the wheel.

Beginners may wish to stay with lower durometers, because the softer wheel will slow them down and give them increased stability. Speed skaters will want higher durometer wheels.

Also consider a wheel's diameter when you buy. Bigger wheels can be difficult for beginners and average skaters. Children may use smaller wheel sizes, perhaps in the high-60-mm range. However, many children can get along fine with adult-size wheels. Far more important than wheel size is the overall fit and comfort of the skate.

Racers often prefer larger wheels, such as 80 mm, especially for outdoor competition. A larger wheel carries the glide farther. Smaller wheels may be used by some skaters in short indoor competitions, such as sprints.

Hockey skates are made to be extra rugged. This model, by Koho, features a lightweight aluminum frame, a replaceable toe cap, and abrasion-resistant materials.

You will notice that the rolling surface (the edge) of some wheels is "pointier" than others'. The pointier the wheel, the faster the glide. Several wheel manufacturers, including Roller Edge Company, offer different edge shapes for different types of skating. Some key differences include:

- A *rounded* edge for skaters who make multiple turns, such as dance performers

- An *elliptical* (more pointed) edge for racing
- A *flatter* edge for recreational skating

Some wheels even have a special construction that makes power or hockey stopping (sideways sliding to a halt) easier. One of these is the 70-mm BrakerWheel, which the company of the same name supplies to Roller Hockey International (RHI), the professional in-line hockey league. This wheel is composed of many rotating disks, which spin around a common hub. Two such wheels are worn on the back two positions of each skate. The makers of BrakerWheel say that this new wheel allows the skater to execute power slides without having to use slower, fatter wheels.

Spacers

Each wheel has a set of bearings in its center. These bearings would slide toward each other with continuing use—and this is the reason spacers exist. They keep the bearings separated. Although there is not much variation in quality, spacers can vary in design, with some having multiple parts.

Bearings

Your skates make use of bearings, which help you roll faster. The type of bearing you use will affect your control, speed, and endurance. Most skaters use either semiprecision bearings or bearings with a low ABEC rating.

ABEC is an acronym standing for Annular Bearing Engineering Council. Low ABEC ratings, such as 1's and 3's are fine for most skaters. Semiprecision bearings will be a drag (literally), so avoid them. Insist on bearings with an ABEC number.

Most bearings are sealed, trapping lubricant inside. This protects the bearings from dust and dirt that will slow down the bearing or ruin it.

Core

The core of many wheels is made of nylon, which weighs less than urethane. Just as bikers want to cut down on the weight of their machines, speed skaters want larger hubs, which require a smaller amount of urethane around them.

BRAKES

You may have one or two brakes on your skates; one is most common. If you're right-handed, it's placed on the heel of the right foot. Brakes are usually made of rubber or urethane, and they bolt into the frame.

Rollerblade Inc. has introduced a special kind of braking technology it calls ABT—which stands for Active Braking Technology. Recognizing that braking remains one of the most critical tasks for beginners to master, Rollerblade has made it easier to come to a halt. ABT works when you slide your braking foot forward. This

Courtesy of Ultra-Wheels

Ultra-Wheels says its patented braking system, called DBS (Disk Braking System), promotes a smoother stop, with less wear and tear on the braking mechanism.

creates pressure on the cuff, which in turn triggers a device in the heel that pushes downward on a brake. The brake descends automatically and touches the ground.

ABT permits the skater to keep all eight wheels on the ground while stopping. This provides more stability than does stopping on just the contact points of four wheels of a back skate, plus a front brake. According to the company, 95 percent of skaters find ABT-equipped skates excellent or acceptable. ABT may be found on several Rollerblade models, including Aeroblade and Coolblade.

Another braking system worth looking into is GRIP In-Line Speed Control. GRIP was the first company to acknowledge that a better stopping device was needed and the first to introduce an advanced brake system. These hand-grip-type brakes can be retrofitted to most any existing in-line skate. Descending from the hand units and linking them with the skates are cords, which control brakes built into two specialized wheels in each skate. The system also includes a "parking brake" feature to facilitate walking.

Some advantages to the GRIP system are:

- It does not wear down like a rubber pad.
- It allows the skater to keep all eight wheels on the ground for stability.
- It enables skaters to control speed on long downhills.

CLOTHING

Choose clothing for comfort and for ability to let you adjust to a changing body temperature. In cooler weather, choose a jacket with a zipper, as opposed to a pullover,

This will allow you to make easy temperature and comfort adjustments. If you are going from one temperature extreme to another, consider wearing a knapsack for the extra clothing you'll shed.

Clothing should not be relied on for safety protection. However, wearing a shirt is a good idea. Skating bare-chested leaves you more exposed to severe road rash, if you bail.

Beyond wearing basic clothing and protective gear, there's no need to bulk up or cover up beyond what feels good. Excellent clothing for the upper body, depending on your preferences, includes tank tops, T-shirts, and button-down shirts. Flexibility and breathability are important considerations. Clothing options for the lower body include bike pants (Lycra Spandex), jeans, shorts, jams (baggy shorts), bathing suits, and sweatpants.

This could be the most important piece of equipment you own.

SAFETY EQUIPMENT

High-quality equipment will be of no benefit to you if you can't skate because of a serious injury. To prevent such an injury, you need to wear protective gear.

Helmets

Skating helmets have no special requirements to distinguish them from biking helmets. However, it's extremely important to *buy* and *use* a *quality helmet*. That means it should be ANSI-, Snell-, or ASTM-approved. *If your hel-met does not have one of these approvals, don't buy it.* Vert and extreme skaters should shop for a helmet that also protects the forehead and the lower part of the neck.

Poorly designed helmets can give the illusion of providing protection. In some ways, this can be worse than no protection at all. You might be tempted to take risks, because you assume that your head is well protected—when it isn't.

The main purpose of your helmet, after all, is to protect your head—the most vulnerable part of your body in skating and just about the only location of a possible fatal injury. Your head is *important*. As succinctly phrased by Valerie Zuver, codirector of the Atlanta to Athens Road Skating Marathon, "It's the only part of your body you can't replace."

Protect your head at all costs. Wear a helmet! Maybe it doesn't seem cool. But being dead or brain-damaged is even less cool.

You will find that most helmets are vented. Don't buy one that is not—you'll swelter in a nonvented model. Also be sure the helmet you choose is strong, light in weight, and comfortable.

Wrist Guards

Next to helmets, wrist guards may be the most important piece of safety gear you wear. Your wrist is a sensitive area. Wrist bones are relatively fragile, and veins are close to the surface. Look for a sturdy plastic structure that protects the underside of your wrists—the part that will hit the road when you extend your hands to protect yourself in a fall.

Not long ago, my 12-year-old son Benjamin showed me two totally carved up wrist guards. He had worn them when taking a particularly bad spill. For both of us, that sight drove home the lesson about the importance of wrist protection.

Elbow Guards

Elbow guards are often left out of the safety mix, but they afford valuable protection for your sensitive elbow joints. Wear them to give yourself an extra margin of protection.

Shred plastic . . .

. . . not skin!

Knee Guards

Fall forward, and you'll most likely fall on your knees. Fall *without* knee guards and your knees will "catch" the road, causing you to tumble out of control. With knee guards, you're likely to leave a nice double-swath of shredded plastic on the road behind you—plastic that would have been your skin. Besides protecting your knees from shredding action, knee guards can also absorb tremendous impact that would otherwise damage your delicate knee joints.

The short of it: wear them!

When shopping for knee guards, look for comfortable Velcro and nylon straps that keep the knee guard from sliding down your leg. Some knee guards give you two options on each guard for keeping them in place: a tube of elastic material that covers the entire back of your knee joint or nylon straps held in place with Velcro. Next to safety, comfort is key in safety gear. So make sure your guards fit well and don't constrict your knees. After all, your knees do considerable flexing when you're skating.

Hip Guards

Hip or bumper guards may seem silly. But for many skaters, they will take some of the sharp edges off the learning curve. For a skater of any age and experience, a broken hip will be a painful, slow-healing injury. Hip protection just makes good sense.

Hockey players will want the extra protection afforded by hip pads. Aggro Sports makes shorts with hip and rear pads built right in, which helps protect the skater who crashes into boards. Skid plates on the shorts help, too—it's far better to slide after a tumble than to roll.

If you've got older friends who are contemplating getting into in-line skating, do them a service by suggesting they get hip guards.

New Wrinkles

Unusual types of skating gear can often enhance the fun of in-line skating. For example, Sled Dogs, or SnowRunners, are flat-bottomed boots that are used for a kind of in-line skating on snow. For them to work well, the snow needs to be hard-packed. For more information, contact SnowRunner.

Windskating is a sport that lays claim to in-line skating, skateboarding, and quad roller skates. You might want to explore this neat, ecologically sound way of covering ground, snow, and ice. Contact Windskate Inc. for more information.

A FINAL WORD ON EQUIPMENT

Skate equipment changes constantly—which is a good thing! Manufacturers are investing a great deal of time and money in improving the sport's hardware—making skating itself safer and more fun. Read skating magazines to check up on new merchandise. Visit your skate shop regularly to see what's new and helpful to your style of skating.

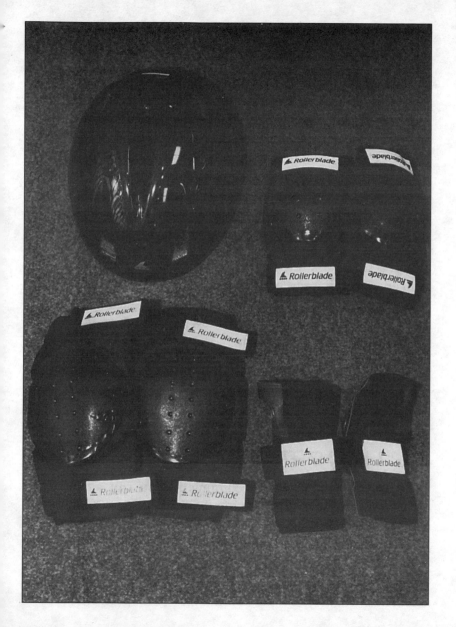

4

SKATING SAFER

*I*n-line skating is a basically safe sport. But that does not mean it's an injury-free sport.

Two factors rank highest in reducing the chance of having an accident: protective gear and the skater's attitude.

Without the right gear and attitude, though, the results can be highly unpleasant. According to the Consumer Product Safety Council (as reported in the *Philadelphia Inquirer*), approximately 83,000 injuries and two deaths were attributed to in-line skating in 1994. That's compared with 37,000 injuries and three deaths in 1993—reflecting the increased popularity of the sport. In 1994, an estimated 49,000 children required attention in emergency rooms. Of these, approximately 23,000 were there with broken bones and 7,000 for potentially more serious head injuries.

If this sounds like a lot of injuries, it is—but not when you consider the number of skating enthusiasts. As Henry Zuver of the International In-Line Skating Association put it:

> When you have 83,000 injuries in a sport with 14,000,000 participants, that's not astronomical—it's about one-half of one percent. But when people wear protective equipment, they dramatically reduce the chance of a severe injury. . . . The one sport that's less dangerous? Fishing! That's according to the National Safety Council and the National Consumer Product Safety Council, using their statistics.

Who takes most of the lumps? Kids do, of course—because they do more skating and are less likely to wear safety gear. Children suffered about 43,000 of the total 1993 in-line injuries.

For those of you who neglect to wear wrist guards, take note: The most common injury was a broken wrist. Bear in mind as well that the most likely fatal injury is a head injury. So if you have to wear only one piece of safety gear, make it a helmet.

Did I scare you a bit? Good!

Gory details and bone-rattling statistics should lead you to skate more safely. There's much you can do and more you ought to know about. This chapter will fill you in on safety basics. (Muscular injuries, dehydration, loss of electrolytes, heat cramps, heat exhaustion, heat stroke, and hypothermia are covered in Chapter 9.)

STEP 1: HAVE A SAFETY-CONSCIOUS ATTITUDE

When a safety-first attitude is maintained, many of the dangers of skating can be removed or reduced. Your best protective measure is under your helmet—it's your mind. Safe skating begins with knowing enough to take only the risks you're ready for.

In the beginning, play it safe. Avoid hills and traffic. Skate on grass or near it. Skate with an experienced skater who can show you the ropes.

STEP 2: WEAR SAFETY GEAR

With the proper protective equipment, you can avoid much of the damage associated with a bad fall. See Chapter 3 for specific advice on gear.

Some first-timers overestimate their stability on skates. They assume that they'll glide with perfect balance. In fact, at the start, maintaining balance can be a challenge. *Right from the beginning*, wear protective gear—buy a complete set in the skate shop, and wear it as you test various brands of skates.

STEP 3: LEARN HOW TO STOP

For the beginner, knowing how to stop is one of the toughest challenges. From a safety standpoint, it's a critical skill. See Chapter 6 to find out about coming to a crawl.

Stopping is so important that skaters actually share their knowledge with beginners in "stopping clinics." In fact, the New York Road Skaters Association has taught thousands of people how to stop. This group has 1,200 members. Of these, 68 have formed the Central Park Skate Patrol, which specializes in giving a hand to beginners. On a single day, the Skate Patrol might teach more than 300 people in Central Park the fine art of rolling to a halt.

With 20,000 to 50,000 skaters in Central Park on any given day, preventing accidents is important—and difficult if only because of the sheer traffic volume. In 1993 alone, the park saw 1,000 in-line skating accidents. Emergency calls appear to be in-line related, too. Ten out of 21 emergencies over one two-day stretch stemmed from in-line accidents. So far, the city government has not imposed a speed limit on skaters, although it has done so with bikers, who are not permitted to go faster than 15 m.p.h. Skaters can reach speeds of 30 m.p.h. or higher.

The point here is not that skating is dangerous, but that it can be risky in a crowded, chaotic environment—especially with beginners abounding. That's why it's critical to have stopping power.

STEP 4: TERRAIN AND SKATING STYLE— KNOW THE LAY OF THE LAND

Work on developing your ability to size up an upcoming stretch of road—it's a skill that will prove valuable. Some skaters make the mistake of underestimating the steepness of a road or the difficulty of handling some tight turns. Sometimes you'll preview the course ahead on foot or by car; other times you'll visually scope it out from a distance before you skate it.

Plan your attack. Maybe you'll slalom a hillside all the way down. Or mix straightaways with slalom turns to lose speed. Figure out how much braking you'll need to do. If there's too much braking in a particular stretch, you may want to skate elsewhere.

Look closely for potholes, rocks, ridges, and gravel—all of which can send you flying. Avoid them—or if that's impossible, take them at slow speed. Also get a sense of the smoothness of the asphalt. Black ice is nice—and fast. That's fine, if you can handle it.

In essence, one of your best measures of protection as a skater is your own knowledge of your skills and how they match up with the path ahead. Judge well, and you'll do fine. But it takes a practiced eye, so work at it. Become a student of the road; it's part of the fun of skating!

©Ari Rosenthal

Know the lay of the land—in this case, West River Drive (Philadelphia). Ari Rosenthal

SKATING NEAR TRAFFIC

Skating on roads, even *busy* roads, remains your right. After all, skating is a *means of transportation*. As skaters, we have to fight for our right to use the paths—the public roads—designed to move people where they want to go.

From a safety standpoint, though, it's best to avoid cars when you can. Your rolling will be more relaxed if you don't have to worry about cars bearing down on you. But avoiding traffic takes some planning. For example, you may want to track down well-paved but little-used side streets that offer easy, relatively safe thrills.

Choose bike paths over roads—when you can find a bike path. That may mean driving to your favorite path. Especially on a weekend, you'll find that it's worth the extra trouble. Your reward will be car-free fun and sights different from those of your everyday routine.

When you do skate on roads, try to use those with soft grass at the roadside. You can never tell when you'll want to bail, and we all love those soft landings! Don't forget to anticipate traffic at intersections—*long* before you approach them. Give yourself plenty of stopping distance, especially if you begin at the top of a hill, and the intersection is in a valley.

When you're forced to skate near traffic, skate on the

than against it. Signal your turns. Stop at stop signs. And don't skate over 55 on interstate highways!

Skating near Pedestrians, Bikers, and Skateboarders

Give pedestrians plenty of room, wherever possible. You'll find that a whistle is useful—announce your approach. And do beware of kids and dogs. They can dart out into your path with no notice. Just expect the unexpected, and you'll be all right!

Bikers, for example, move so fast and come up on you so quickly that they can cause serious problems. Let them pass you on your left. Skateboarders will give you less of a problem. Likewise, just give them plenty of berth.

right. Give yourself at least a yard of room to your right. This way, if a car passes too close to you, you'll have some breathing room for shifting rightward while managing not to hit the curb.

Laws

Obey traffic regulations and local laws pertaining to skating. That means skating *with* the flow of traffic, rather

Jumping over squad cars can have serious consequences.

It helps to have a common understanding of which group should be traveling on which side of the road. In Central Park, some progress has been made on this front—the unwritten rule is that bicyclists hug the outside lane, and runners use the inside lane. Skaters sandwich themselves in between.

Everyone should remember one basic principle: Be courteous. Let others pass if they want to pass. Concede an extra inch or foot to others for more comfortable pass-

Always be on the lookout for cyclists.

ing. Smile, and you'll feel better. If it's in you, say "How ya doin'?" or toss out your favorite friendly greeting. You'll get plenty of smiles in return, it will cost you nothing, and you'll have a better time!

The International In-Line Skating Association has compiled its own set of safety rules (see page 37), endorsed by major skating manufacturers. These rules give you another handy way of viewing the essentials of safety.

A WORD TO PARENTS

Parents, you can do a great deal to keep your children skating safely. Follow these basic suggestions:

1. Insist that your children wear protective gear, including a helmet and wrist, knee, and elbow guards.

2. Understand the kinds of challenges your kids are attempting. Learn enough about the sport to know whether they are trying a move, a hill, or a course that's way beyond their reach. But recognize that some element of risk taking is inherent in all sports.

3. Be sure your children get and use quality equipment.

4. Don't let your kids skate in or near traffic; on icy, snowy, or graveled roads; on steep hills; or at night without adult supervision.

Parents!—teach your kids safe skating.

THE IISA RULES OF THE ROAD

1. Wear all protective equipment.

2. Stay alert and be courteous at all times.

3. Control your speed.

4. Skate on the right side of paths, trails, and sidewalks.

5. Overtake other pedestrians, cyclists, and skaters on the left. Use extra caution and announce your intention by saying, "Passing on your left." Pass only when it is safe and when you have enough room for both of you to be at the full extension of your stride.

6. Be aware of changes in trail conditions due to traffic, weather conditions, and hazards such as water, potholes, or storm debris. When in doubt, slow down. Do not skate on wet or oily surfaces.

7. Obey all traffic regulations. When on skates, you have the same obligations as a moving vehicle.

8. Stay out of areas with heavy automobile traffic.

9. Always yield for pedestrians.

10. Before using any trail, achieve a basic skating level, including the ability to turn, control speed, brake on downhills, and recognize and avoid skating obstacles.

IISA Rules of the Road provided courtesy of the International In-Line Skating Association. For further information on IISA, call 1-404-728-9707.

HOW TO FALL

Falling doesn't have to be a big part of your experience, even at the beginning. But because just about everyone falls sometimes, it's important to be mentally and physically prepared.

Sometimes you'll have a measure of control over how you fall, and sometimes you won't. The guidelines that follow apply when you do have some way of anticipating and controlling what happens.

The best way to fall is *with* your falling motion rather than against it. Put another way, it's better to slide than to roll. If you can fall and slide on the plastic surfaces of your safety gear, you stand a better chance of avoiding injury than if you roll. Your wrist guards have protruding hard structures that help contain the impact of a fall and allow you to slide. If you have time to react before a fall:

1. Extend your arms and land on your knees and wrists.

2. Land with the impact hitting on your wrist and knee guards—to the extent you can maneuver this.

3. Leave a cool trail of plastic in your wake.

4. Arise and smile!

A Falling Summary

- If you are out of control, roll with your motion rather than fight the tendency of your body to keep moving.

- Should you have a choice of bailing zones, choose the softer ones: grass over gravel, sand over asphalt.

- To *reduce* your chance of falling badly and hurting yourself: avoid gravel, sand, bad roads, pedestrians, and traffic; skate within the range of your ability; and move at a comfortable speed.

- Lastly, expect to fall—especially when learning new tricks. It's part of learning!

5

MAINTENANCE

Keeping your skates in good shape is easy and well worth the small investment in your time. Maintaining your skates involves checking your skates and safety equipment regularly, cleaning everything, and lubricating where appropriate.

Before heading out to skate, always give your equipment the once-over.

THE BASIC SAFETY CHECK

1. *Wheels.* Check for uneven wear. Rotate or replace wheels if necessary. Spin the wheels, checking for dirt on the wheels themselves and in the hub.

2. *Frame/chassis.* Check the frame for damage, including cracks and loose grommets.

3. *Buckles.* Be sure they fasten well. Buckles can be replaced—by you or by an attendant at a skate shop.

4. *Safety gear.* Check your helmet and knee, elbow, and wrist guards for excessive wear and breaks.

MAINTAINING AND ROTATING YOUR WHEELS

Wheels may be relatively expensive, but you shouldn't have to replace them very often.

When your wheels become worn more on one side than the other, it's time to rotate them. The main goal of rotation is to even out the rate of wear on your wheels, to make them last longer, and to keep your skating smooth.

Theories and methods of rotating wheels vary widely. I will offer you an individualized approach and a generalized one.

An *individualized* way of rotating your wheels is to look for the ones that are worn down the most. Use a caliper or a ruler to determine which wheels are largest and smallest. If you're skating properly, most of your weight will be on your heels, so your rearmost wheels should be the most beat up. Move your largest wheels into the rear position. These should also be the wheels in the best condition. When rotating your wheels, be sure to face the most worn side outside—facing away from your other foot. Typically, the inner edge (the side that faces your other foot) will wear down the fastest. That's why you want to check each wheel for wear as part of the rotation procedure. Place the edge that is worn down the most on the outside this time. By doing so, you will extend the life of your wheels (deferring your next $100 bill for eight new wheels).

For a *generalized* approach to rotating (because you prefer to follow a simple system), begin by lining up your

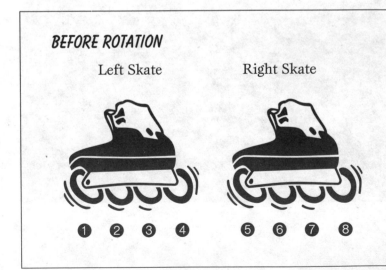

BEFORE ROTATION

Left Skate   Right Skate

① ② ③ ④   ⑤ ⑥ ⑦ ⑧

Rotate wheels from one skate to the other to reduce uneven wear.

skates side by side. Remove all of your wheels and label them 1 to 8. Move your wheels in the pattern shown in the illustration. *Do not flip your wheels as you move them.* By moving them as shown in the illustration, you will automatically be shifting all inside edges to outside edges and vice versa.

Removing and Replacing Wheels

Removing wheels can be a little messy. It's best to wear old clothes or to put a rag on your lap. Also have a surface nearby where you can lay out your wheels in proper order as you remove them.

To remove your wheels:

1. Hold a skate in wheels-up position between your knees.

2. Unscrew your wheels with the right tool for your particular skates: Allen wrench, adjustable or socket wrench, or a manufacturer-provided tool.

3. Check your bearings and wheels for dirt, and clean them by removing them and wiping them

AFTER ROTATION

Left Skate Right Skate

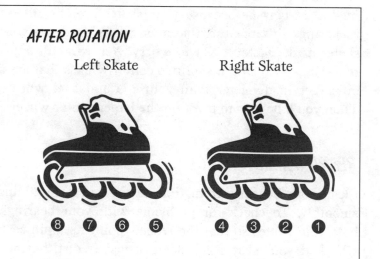

⑧ ⑦ ⑥ ⑤   ④ ③ ② ①

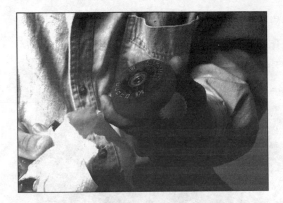

down with a cloth. Because bearings are usually sealed or shielded, this wipe-down should do the job. If you feel your bearings have dirt inside them, clean the bearings (see the section on bearing maintenance).

4. Replace wheels. Don't overtighten your new wheels—keeping them snugly secure will be fine.

Rockering

Some skaters like to be able to turn, pivot, or change directions quickly. "Rockering" your wheels makes it easier. This term refers to the lowering of your middle wheels so that they are the ones making most of the contact with the ground. (Skate dancers find the rockered position especially helpful.) On a five-wheeled skate, you would rocker the middle three wheels; on a four-wheeled skate, the middle two; and on a three-wheeled skate, the center wheel only.

To rocker your skates, you must remove from the exterior side of the chassis the wheels and the center spacer that separates the two bearings. The position of the axle in the different holes or cutouts in the chassis determines whether your wheel is in a flat position or rockered. Move the center spacer to the desired lower position and reattach your bolts and wheels. You may need to turn your spacer upside down to fit it in the rockered position.

Be prepared for a surprise when you first ride rockered wheels. You will probably feel unsteady at first, so hold onto something solid, such as a railing.

Can't find an extra set of holes or cutouts for rockering? That may be because your skates aren't built for rockering—it's a feature that must be designed into your skates at the factory. Not to worry! You can still enjoy rockering—buy and install two center wheels that are a bit larger in diameter than your toe and heel wheels. Then you'll be able to pivot on the larger center wheels.

BEARING MAINTENANCE

Clean your bearings from time to time to keep gliding smoothly. To check for problems with your bearings, hold your skates so that the wheels point up. Spin each wheel. If your skates are clean of visible dirt, but any wheel moves slowly, you may have bearing problems.

Your bearings may need cleaning long before your wheels need replacing. The frequency of cleanings will depend on how much dirt you gather on a typical outing. Also, speed skaters usually spend more time cleaning and lubricating so that they will be able to skate as fast as possible.

The best time to clean your bearings is (you guessed it) when you're cleaning your wheels. Why make two messes when you can get by with only one? It's the nittiest, grittiest phase of skate maintenance, but somebody's got to do it—and it may as well be you. The silver lining is that going through the process will help familiarize you with how your skates work.

Smart idea: clean your bearings outdoors so that the fumes from your spray lubricant will dissipate into the open air. Otherwise, use a room with plenty of ventilation.

Here's what you'll need:

- A can of lubricating and cleaning product (such as WD-40)
- A set of rags and paper towels
- A screwdriver (preferably Phillips-head) or bearing-removal tool
- An Allen wrench—4 mm for most skates—or a manufacturer-supplied tool

And here's the procedure:

1. Use a 4-mm Allen wrench or other tool to remove one end of the axle.
2. Remove the outside spacer.
3. Use the angled part of the Allen wrench (or a stubby screwdriver) to pry out the bearing. If you gradually pry out the bearing in a series of moves while rotating the wheel in your hand, you can avoid gouging the bearing or other parts.
4. Turn the wheel upside down, and the center spacer will fall out.

5. Use a fat tool, such as the handle of a screwdriver or a small, wide-shanked screwdriver, to push out the second bearing and the outside spacer.

6. Take both bearings in one hand. Spray both bearings with lubricant. Wipe them hard with a dry cloth. Lubricate the wheel hub by spraying it. Try to keep the surface of the wheel dry—if you wet it, wipe it clean.

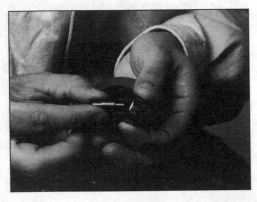

7. Clean the spacer retainers with a cotton swab and lubricant. Also clean the chassis interior and exterior.

8. Reinsert the inside and center spacers, then the outside spacer.

9. Reinsert the axle ends, female first. Then twist the male ends into position, while holding the female still with a second Allen wrench. Or you can twist both wrenches simultaneously. Make the fit snug, but not tight.

Now just test the spinning ability of each bearing, place them all back in your skates, and you're ready to roll again. That's all there is to the dirtiest job in skating!

REPLACING BRAKES

When your brake even looks worn, replace it—whether or not you're sure you can get a few more stops out of it. If you struggle even the slightest bit to make solid contact with the road, there's no doubt whatsoever that your old brake has given up the ghost. Remember that aside from wearing a helmet and using common sense, your ability to STOP is your most precious safety asset.

Brakes are not expensive. Most are made of urethane, a screw, and sometimes a rigid polypropylene structure. No matter what kind of brake you have, most times you'll find it's easy to replace. A screwdriver will usually do it.

Occasionally, replacing a brake proves to be a real bear. Not long ago, I found that my worn brake was all

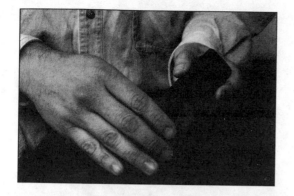

but unremovable. I tried using screwdrivers, power screwdrivers, chisels, a tire iron, and various lubricants. The urethane had apparently fused around the retaining screw. The only remedy? The services of a devoted skate shop proprietor, who used grinding tools and powerful saws to hack away at the obstinate brake. The lesson for you here—get help from a pro who has the tools and experience to do the job.

A Final Word About Brake Maintenance

On many skates, brakes can be switched from the right to the left skate. Also a second brake can be added, so that both skates have brakes.

Procedures vary by skate manufacturer and the designs used. Often, the brake is attached to a housing that attaches to the rear axle and to a notch in the rear heel. In general, the brake can be switched by detaching the nuts, removing the axle, bearings, and spacers, and pulling the brake housing out from under the heel. Then you switch the position of this entire apparatus from the right skate to the left skate. The left wheel and associated parts in turn move to the right skate.

Note that a larger axle is often used to secure the braking wheel. So if you want two brakes—one per foot—you would need to order a second larger axle.

6

FIRST MOVES

You'll be moving fast soon enough—so take it slow at first!

Many people make the mistake of thinking that because in-line skating looks easy, they can just put on skates and roll down a slope. They often end up with a bruised tailbone—or worse. Just as you wouldn't sky-dive before getting an on-the-ground lesson, so you wouldn't want to go flying down a steep hill during your first in-line outing. Make your first moves under the safest conditions.

This chapter will show you how to feel your balance, get rolling, stop, and turn. These are your basics. Take your time learning them, and you'll roll far!

WHAT YOU MAY WISH TO UNLEARN

In-line skating is definitely its own sport. It's not exactly like ice skating, old-style roller skating, or skateboarding. Because you might be carrying over some of your old habits and perceptions from these other sports, let's see where these could help or hurt you.

A Word for Ice-Skaters

In-line skating is very similar to ice skating, but some of the differences are worth noting.

You're probably more likely to fall on in-line skates, because there's always a pebble or twig to watch out for, which isn't the case on smooth ice. When you do fall, the street is harder than ice. Asphalt will cut you worse than ice will—so wearing safety gear is even more important.

In-line skating is also often *faster* than ice skating. That's because you frequently go down hills, gaining speed. Think about it—no ice-skater ever goes downhill.

Stopping can be different, too—you can't power stop as easily on pavement by using your skate's edges. It is certainly possible, but only if you're very skilled.

In ice skating, you can make a snowplow stop. This is accomplished by bending at the waist, spreading your legs, and angling your toes inward, and your heels outward. As you'll see later in this chapter, this stop is possible to do with in-line skates, but it's harder. Snow gives way to skis and ice to blades more easily than asphalt does to wheels moving sideways.

In ice skating, many people go around in circles—but with in-line skates you can go anywhere and in almost any weather. Ice is more slippery, so the *feel* of your riding surface is different.

You're also more *secure* on in-line skates. I personally find that in-line skates give you more support and comfort than do ice skate boots, which are usually made of leather and a light lining. Some ice-skaters would dispute this, saying that a well-fitted figure skating boot made of stiff leather gives excellent support.

In some ways, ice skates give you more control than in-lines, and in other ways, less. They give more control in moves involving the toe pick, which is absent from in-lines. The toe pick is used to control speed during backward skating and to allow the skater to do toe jumps and toe jump landings. The ice-skater moving to in-line will have to find other approaches or solutions to these moves. Some helpful ideas are provided in Chapter 12.

Many of the turns and moves of ice skating, such as crossovers and backward skating, are done similarly on in-line skates. If you can perform these moves on ice, you should have no problem doing them on in-line skates, but you should be *careful* when first trying out any old moves. Because ice just *feels* different from asphalt, you'll definitely notice a difference that will affect your balance and timing.

With ice skates, you're sliding and can't get a grip on anything. With in-line skates, you have more control. So take it slow at first, knowing that, ultimately, this new sport will prove easier.

If You're an Experienced Traditional Roller Skater

The main challenge when moving from traditional roller skates to in-lines lies in getting a feel for the edges of your wheels. At first, just rock back and forth and side to side to get your balance. The old quad-style four wheels gave you a more secure platform—you had more support than you do now. Expect that in-line skating will be different and that balancing will take more work.

But there are some benefits you'll love—*it's easier to go fast* on in-line skates. You'll come to love the speed and the effortlessness of your glide. And if you're into moves and stunts, you've come to the right sport. Having wheels all in a row will mean some extra work for you at first, but stick with it and you'll find the new skates help you to increase your flexibility and agility. This is different and (if you're like most roller skaters who try in-line) more rewarding.

Skateboarders, Take Note—This Is Different!

One of the major differences between skateboarding and in-line skating is that you can't jump off your skates the way you can a skateboard. That means you've got to be more careful about taking chances. An example: you see an object in your path. A skateboarder can decide to dodge the object and easily go scampering away *on foot* in a new direction. Not so for in-liners.

Skateboarders first trying in-line skates need to take things on especially slowly at first—and not assume that being a great thrasher also makes someone a great in-line

skater. In-line skates have no trucks (the angle-shifting axles on skateboards) to lean on for changes of direction and balance. On the positive side, you'll find that you can get a better workout with in-line skating. Also, in many ways you'll have more control. Welcome to a more aerobic, muscle-building sport.

WHERE TO LEARN

You can start off right by beginning on a flat surface. Grass is best—fall on your duff, and all you get is a grass stain! Grass gives you good cushioning for your first falls and it also prevents you from rolling out of control. Beginning on grass is especially smart if you've never roller-skated, skateboarded, or ice-skated before. At least you'll get a feeling for the skates and a sense of balance on a low-risk surface.

Wherever you choose to make your first roll, be sure it's a flat surface. You want to be in control while you're learning.

Start on grass.

Some choice spots for your first outing, in order of preference:

- A lawn
- A baseball field
- A quiet park
- A carpeted floor
- A school yard
- A tennis court
- A quiet street

If you choose to skate at first on grass—as I recommend—try to find a stretch of lawn that's even, dry, and large. Short grass will keep you rolling a bit better than long grass.

When learning on a tennis court, touch the fence for support. On a quiet street you can likewise reach out to lean on a tree, a fence, or a railing. You may even want to have an experienced skater hold your arm or hand when you first start out.

Wherever you choose to learn, however, be sure to keep twigs, dirt, and other debris out of the path of your skates as much as possible.

Take a Course—Learn from Someone Who Knows

IISA, USAC/RS, and NIHA have instructor-certification programs. Skaters who have passed their certification have a great deal to offer you, even if you've been on skates and think you know the fundamentals.

At one time, it was possible to list all of the nation's certified instructors in a book like this. Now, because the sport has grown so amazingly, such a list would take up a book in itself!

Not to worry—call or write to IISA, USAC/RS, or NIHA (see Appendix A for addresses and phone numbers), and they'll guide you to a local expert. They may even be able to guide you to an expert in a specialty that interests you, such as racing, in-line hockey, artistic skating, or extreme and vert skating.

Learn at a Roller Rink? It Depends

It's not the wisest idea, but some people choose to learn in-line skating at a commercial skating rink. The problem with a rink is that wood and cement floors are less forgiving than grass. Bumping into other skaters is another difficulty.

A rink *does* offer some advantages, though. In winter, you stay warm. Dirt, potholes, and stones can't rough up your roll. And, of course, you can hold onto that helpful side railing.

Most rinks do not rent in-line skates, though they will allow some skaters who bring their own to use them. The reason for their refusal to rent? Bolts (wheel axles) on some skates scratch their floors. But with the newer models of skates, rink owners' attitudes toward in-line skates should change. These newer skates are being made with flattened bolts so that they can be used at rinks.

When you do start out, wear your safety gear: knee pads, elbow pads, gloves, and a helmet. Consider hip pads, too, for that extra measure of protection. They're relatively new on the market, but they make very good sense. If you're a beginner, you're more likely than an advanced skater to need the extra hip protection, since you're more likely to fall. And advanced skaters who are trying new tricks—such as ramp moves and stair riding—should welcome this extra safety margin while learning.

Before heading out, make sure your skates are reasonably snug—close-fitting but not pinching. Your buckles or laces should also feel snug and help your upper boot give you firm support. In-line skates give you a good deal of ankle support, which will help keep you upright.

WARM-UP STRETCHES

Do these exercises before you head out to skate. They will help limber you up and reduce your chances of pulling a muscle.

Groin Stretch

1. Begin in a standing position, with your legs spread far apart.
2. Bend one leg at the knee to a 90-degree angle. Position your upper body over this leg. Place your other leg out to the side.

Groin stretch.

3. Stretch out your sideways-extended thigh. Accentuate the stretching by pushing down with a hand on your upper thigh. You should feel a pull on the insides of your thighs. These are your groin muscles.
4. Repeat by switching positions and outstretching the other leg. Do one groin stretch per leg.

Toe Touches

1. Stand with legs together and toes pointed up.
2. Lean down and forward.
3. Actually grab onto your toes. Hold on to them for approximately 30 seconds. Do it just once.

Toe touches.

Sitting toe touches.

Sitting Toe Touches

1. Sit with your legs spread apart.
2. Touch your left foot.
3. Move your hands to the middle area between your legs.
4. Finally, grab the toes of your right foot. Hold for a few seconds.

Your Quack Act: The Duck Walk

This may sound strange. To learn how to skate, walk like a duck. Why? You'll get a feel for the skates while still maintaining maximum control. Put on your skates. Point your toes to the side. Bend slightly at the waist. Place one foot in front of the other, stride forward, and walk like a duck. This is also known as a V-walk. You may not realize it, but you're learning some moves you'll use later in actual skating.

Duck walk around on the grass. . . . Feeling comfortable on your skates yet? After a while, you should begin feeling capable and in control on your skates.

YOU'RE READY FOR STROKING

Like good freestyle dancing, the secret of skating is *getting down*. You want to lean forward slightly. That will bring your shin against the tongue of your skate—it's like skiing. Keep your knees bent. Feel your weight on the inner edge of your wheels—that's where it should be. Now here's the basic move:

1. Push off with one foot, shoving behind you and outward to the side. This gives you the traction you need to get going.

2. Move your weight over your leading foot.

3. Swing your opposite arm forward. For example, if you're stroking forward with your left foot, your right arm should be swinging *in front* of you.

Get low to stroke.

Reverse position and swing with your other arm and foot. Maintain your crouch. Push off and to the side with your trailing foot. Go for a rhythm that's comfortable for you.

Congrats! You're *stroking!* Work up a rhythm on the grass. Get the feel of your stroke. It gets easier, doesn't it?

Don't get overconfident now; you're just skating on grass. Sure, you've mastered a basic move. But it's easy to stop on grass—all you have to do is stop stroking. Asphalt will be more difficult.

Work on your stroke until you get it down. Consider yourself into it just for the sweat right now—the thrills of speed and torque will come along soon enough.

Skate on *all* of your wheels, except when your skate is off the ground. Consciously stroke with the entire set of wheels touching the ground. This will give more power to your moves and maintain your stability.

Get Bent

Standing straight up is the quickest way of falling right down. You want to keep your knees bent just a bit and your upper body angled slightly forward at all times when skating. Don't lock your knees—that decreases your flexibility and ability to shift weight quickly.

STOP!

Sure, you just got started. But this is the best time to learn how to stop. For without stopping power, you're just one out-of-control mass of rolling flesh.

In skating, bent is beautiful.

CHOOSE YOUR STOPS

Type of Stop	Best Use
Stopping on a slowing surface	Leaving a sidewalk or bike path, exiting to a lawn
Turning to a stop	Reaching the end of a wide skating area, such as a parking lot or wide street
Heel stop	On a flat surface or an easy downhill, for a gradual stop
T-stop	For a relatively abrupt stop (hard to do—wears down your wheels)
Snowplow	For a gradual stop, at moderate speeds
Power stop or hockey stop	For experts only: for use in roller hockey and in unexpected emergency situations

Here's good news for you—there are at least six great ways of stopping (see table). Learn several of these stops, then use the ones that are right for each situation.

Skate onto a Slowing Surface

You don't always have the option of slowing down by entering a slowing surface—but it can be fun. One option is leaving asphalt for lawn. If you fall, it's no big deal. You probably won't break any bones.

Extend your hands for balance, bend at the knees, and get ready for irregular rolling and bumps. If you do hit a bump, run a few steps and do what you can to keep from falling.

In a slightly different approach, the IISA recommends that beginners riding onto grass to stop get in the ready position for a heel stop—but without actually braking when hitting the grass. Instead, the skater rolls with one foot extended and one foot in normal position, with hands spread and in front of the body.

Try both methods, and use the one that works best for you.

Avoid skating off asphalt onto a dirt path—dirt gets stuck in your wheels, as you'll quickly learn. Be careful about skating on cement or gravel paths. Those surfaces will not only wear down your wheels quickly but will also make you more likely to fall.

Another slowing option is simply to head up onto an inclined area, such as a driveway or street on a hillside.

Turning to a Stop

This way of slowing is simple at slow speeds. Turn in a circle and slow down. If you're headed down an incline, you can do a 180-degree turn and come to a complete halt while headed uphill. Making a wide turn to a stop is a variation on the glide turn, covered on page 57. Or you may wish to do a 360-degree turn. This will slow you down but leave you headed in the same direction.

Heel Stop

Unlike a regular roller skate, which has a brake before the toe, an in-line skate has its brake at the back. Usually, only one skate has this brake, and most often it's the right skate, because most people feel more comfortable braking with the right foot.

Let's run through the heel stop, assuming your brake is on your right foot and you're gliding along, your feet slightly apart:

The heel stop.

1. Lean slightly forward, placing most of your weight on your left foot. Extend your hands in front of you. This will help protect you in case of a fall, as well as give you more balancing capability.

2. Place your right leg forward (the brake foot) so that your right heel is close to the toe of your left foot.

3. Bend your knees and point your right toe upward—which positions your heel downward to drag lightly on the brake.

Nick Perna shows how turning to a stop can be done in a fluid, even way.

Courtesy of Michelle and Nick Perna

4. Move your body weight forward, increasing the downward pressure on your right foot until you stop. Your left (nonbraking) foot should bear most of your body weight.

This stop is a great friend of the skater. Sometimes—say, when you're going a bit faster than you want to on a downhill—this is the stopper you want in your repertoire.

The faster you're moving, the harder this stop is to execute without losing balance. You will sense the appropriate amount of pressure you need to place on your right foot—the amount you can handle and still keep your balance. Practice at slow speeds to gain confidence.

You can also use your heel stop to slow down, rather than stop completely. For instance, on a bike path on a long hill, you can't easily turn uphill to decrease speed (the path is too narrow). Heel braking in a series of tap-like motions becomes your best bet for slowing down.

T-Stop

The T-stop is one of the most popular ways of stopping. It can also help you make a tight turn in some situations. Drag either foot behind you, at a perpendicular angle, making the "T" that gives the move its name. Your dominant foot should be the trailing one:

The T-stop.

1. Lift your trailing foot and place it behind your leading foot, but perpendicular to it (making a T-shape).

2. Bend at your waist and knees.

3. Drag the wheels of your trailing foot on its inside wheel edges. Keep most of your weight on your leading foot. Use all of your trailing foot wheels for maximum stopping power.

This stop demands thigh strength. It's harder to do than a heel stop, but it can be a handy addition to your slowing-down repertoire.

Zak Hoffstein shows a side view of the heel stop.

Try it at a crawl, and then build up until you really burn rubber (urethane)!

Snowplow

This stop can work well at slower speeds. Some skaters find that they prefer this stop—it's easier and more comfortable for them. Try it and see if this is one you like, too.

1. Glide, and then allow your feet to form a slight V pattern until they're comfortably apart.
2. Angle your toes inward, while gently applying pressure to the inside edges of your wheels.

This pressure will help you stop. With enough outward pressure, your feet may not come any closer than a foot apart (in an adult).

Power Stop

The toughest stop to master is the power stop. It's the hardest to execute, but quickest to bring you to a total halt.

My advice: Learn this one with somebody who's mastered it. It's a good idea to ask an ice hockey player to help you, since that's the sport where this move was developed. Better yet, find an in-line hockey player who's mastered this tough move.

Here's how to do the power stop:

1. Bend at the waist and knees. (The next two steps happen very quickly.)
2. Turn either left or right, leading with your dominant foot.

©Art Rosenthal

A power stop outside the Philadelphia Art Museum.

3. Extend your leading foot in front of you, but now place it at a sharp angle—almost sideways.
4. Tilt your body backward, to keep from flipping over your leading foot.
5. Press down hard with your leading foot, so that your inner edge meets the pavement.

Your stopping angle must be sharp to avoid flipping over your leading foot and taking a nasty fall. Twisting an ankle is also possible.

Ice hockey players need to stop on a dime, to be able to chase the puck. In-line skaters who don't play hockey usually don't require this abruptness. Still, it is a good emergency move to have in your bag of tricks. It can come in handy if a car pops out of nowhere or if you suddenly find an unexpected obstacle, hole, bump, cyclist, or pedestrian right in front of you.

TURNING

After a while, skating straight ahead becomes pretty boring. Consider the nature of the rest of life:

- Roads curve.
- Hills curve upward and have curved sides.
- Life throws us curves!

Courtesy of Michelle and Nick Perna

The slalom turn, or hockey glide, provides you with a graceful way of practicing your turns.

In-line skating imitates life (and is a part of it). So let's take some turns together. There are basically two moves to learn: the glide and the crossover.

Glide Turn

1. Lean a little lower than you would for straight-ahead skating.
2. Bend your knees.
3. Lean into the direction you want to turn.
4. Place your lead foot (the one closer to the direction you want to turn) a half-step in front of your trailing foot.
5. Position your body weight over your leading foot.

You'll be riding on the outer edge of your leading foot and on the inner edge of your trailing foot.

Before long, you'll find glide turning easy. Keep practicing. Tighter or higher-speed curves will require more balance, which you'll acquire, as long as you keep at it!

Crossover Turn

Now that you've managed basic turning, you might try the more difficult crossover. This move doesn't slow you down. You can even speed up while turning.

The move is well-known to ice- and roller skaters, and it helps them gain speed while turning. Now you, too, are ready to increase power while changing direction. You'll be able to do it, with practice. The instructions that follow use a left turn. For executing a right crossover, simply substitute the word "left" for "right." Practice on flat, even ground, with plenty of room for turning.

The basic maneuver involves crossing one foot over the other, as you make the turn.

1. Skate and turn left.
2. Ride the outer edge of your left skate.
3. Lean left with your upper body while keeping arms extended to the right side and forward.
4. Move your left leg behind you while moving out to the right. Push to gain thrust.
5. Simultaneously bring your right leg forward, crossing over in front of you and over and to the left.
6. Plant your right skate down and transfer your weight to that foot.
7. Bring up your left foot and skate straight, or repeat for more crossover turning.

You can keep crossing over to build up speed and to turn faster and harder. Keep your hands in front of you and your knees bent while performing this maneuver. If you're right-handed, it's easier to turn left in a crossover. But don't ignore learning the opposite direction, whether you're right- or left-handed.

The more moves you can perform easily, the more fun you'll have. Also, you'll be able to skate on different terrain with greater grace and confidence.

SUMMING UP

There, you've got the basics! Now master them.

Try out new landscapes—bike paths, quiet roads, paved trails on hillsides. You'll find your own special skating spots. My personal favorite—an unused parking lot on a hillside. In my neighborhood, we have a high school parking lot that's perfectly empty of cars on weekends.

I sometimes head out with my kids and friends, all loaded into a station wagon crammed with in-line skate gear, skateboards, bicycles, slalom cones, and refreshments. It's a welcome change from road and trail scenes.

We have a beautiful day in the sun, and I'm just a rollin' fool.

Skate on!

7

ADVANCED MOVES

*T*he tricks described in this chapter vary in difficulty; the easier moves are described first. Read about them all. Then try them when and if you're ready. Warning: you may get ideas!

HOW TO HAVE FUN ON HILLS

In a few places, such as large paved parking lots on hillsides, you may be able to traverse the hill, or slalom. You can work on your slalom style and on

59

Warning: Do not attempt the following tricks without expert, professional instruction. Neither the author nor the publisher assumes responsibility for any injury incurred by a skater attempting these or any other moves described in this book.

Anywhere Sports Productions

crossover turns, as you change directions while descending. Scout out such a place in your neighborhood. You'll have a ball.

Taking Steep Downhills

There are two ways to handle intense downhills: skating tuck-style and criss-crossing the hill.

Gliding Tuck-Style Downhill

On a hill and feeling adventurous? Get into a tuck position and roll with the slope. To do this safely, you need all of the protective gear known to humanity, plus an assurance that no cars or pedestrians will interfere. Finally, you need a straightaway or an upward incline ahead to enable you to slow down.

When you're headed down a steep hill and going for maximum speed (or simply rolling with the gravity), here's how to tuck-glide:

1. Bend deeply at the knees and waist.
2. Keep your hands in front of you and slightly to the side.
3. Spread your legs about 8–12 inches apart.

Criss-crossing Hills

A slower and safer way of taking steep hills is to traverse or criss-cross them. On a narrow downhill road, this may be difficult: The narrower the road, the sharper the turns you have to make as you approach the curb or roadside. When taking your first hills, look not only for a wide road, but also for one with grass on its sides—so you can bail with ease.

To criss-cross a wide road on a hill:

1. Move into a sideways glide across the hill.
2. Make a sharp turn toward the downhill direction as you approach the edge of the road. On a wide hill, you can even head uphill a bit to reduce speed.
3. Cross the hill or road in the opposite direction.
4. Repeat as often as you like.

Heading Uphill

Skating uphill not only takes more work but also builds your leg muscles and gives you a good workout. Another positive result is that your ability to handle uphills and downhills helps you use in-line skating as genuine *transportation*. It's part of your assurance that you can get where you are going, no matter what terrain lies ahead.

Let's assume you're beginning on flat land. Here's how to take that big hill ahead of you:

1. Skate hard and gain speed on flat land. This will keep you going.
2. As the hill gets steeper, your strokes will get shorter.

3. Keep your arms extended and forward.
4. Bend at the waist.
5. Use side-to-side arm and torso motions to gain forward thrust.
6. As the hill gets yet steeper, shorten your strides again.
7. When the hill threatens to stop you, skate in a more duck or V-walk position. Use the inner edges of your wheels for pushing power.

ROCK 'N' ROLL

An alternative way to start rolling is to rock 'n' roll, rather than stride or push off. All you need to do is skate, slide, then angle your legs in parallel, at about a 45-degree angle. Change the angles of your skates from leaning left to leaning right, and repeat, swaying back and forth. Use upper and lower body English (swaying motions of the arms and movements of the torso) to help propel your body forward.

HOURGLASSING (SCULLING) FRONTWARD

Try this move first on a flat landscape. Skate in a pattern that leaves an imaginary hourglass-shaped trail behind you.

1. Roll with your heels together.

2. Point your toes outward, allowing your legs to spread apart in a V-shape.

3. Then point your toes inward.

4. Repeat.

The angle of your legs will change, as you spread your legs outward and then draw them inward. Keep your center of gravity low and your arms extended in front of you and slightly outward.

Work at your rhythm; take it slow at first. Graduate to a slightly downward inclined road surface. You'll actually find it easier there as you make gravity work for you.

HOURGLASSING (SCULLING) BACKWARD

Check out the land behind you before you begin and also as you move.

1. Start with your toes together.

2. Begin a backward stride, slowly at first. Place both skates on the ground.

3. Point your heels away from each other (outward). Spread your legs apart, and draw them back together again.

Admittedly easier said than done! But it is doable.

SKATING ON TOES

The objective in this move is to skate on both of your toes—one wheel per skate. For this description, we'll assume that your right foot is your forward one:

1. Begin by striding, then simply rolling.

2. Transfer your weight to the front toe of your right foot.

3. Tilt the heel of the right foot so that it's up off the ground. You're up on one toe now. . . . Be careful but keep going! Your left foot remains on the ground. Increase the amount of body weight on the angled toe of your right foot.

4. This is the hard part. Now tilt your left foot in the same way so that you're up on the toes of both skates. You've done it!

DAFFY

This move is a variation on skating on your toes—actually it's skating on one heel and one toe, with legs spread:

1. Stride, roll, and extend one leg forward, so that you're rolling on the heel of that foot. Keep your back leg bent.

2. Slowly lift the heel of your back foot.

3. Spread your legs apart. Now you're daffying.

© Arl Rosenthal

The daffy.

CURB JUMP

Attempt this move only where in accordance with the law.

Practice your first jumps nowhere near a curb! Why take a chance when you're first taking to the air? Pick a smooth, flat surface; put on all your safety gear; and then:

1. Stride and roll. Extend your arms in front of you, for balance and to catch yourself if you fall.

2. About 10 feet before your launching point, place one leg in front of the other and crouch.

3. Finally, jump, land—and keep your balance.

Got it? Now do it a few more times on flat ground. When you're ready for your first curb, pick a low one with flat, even cement above it—or better yet, cement followed by grass for a soft, preplanned fall, such as in a public park.

Gradually, you'll be able to take higher curbs. One way to practice taking to the air is to jump over a row of slalom cones. Hit one, and it will simply tip over without tripping you into a bad fall. Learning to jump curbs will enable you to handle certain city skating situations with ease.

AGGRESSIVE AND STREETSTYLE SKATING

This form of skating is an attitude as much as it is a specialized group of moves. Aggressive skating can be considered the same as streetstyle skating, although some skaters may not agree.

Body Moves

To get air and to execute various moves, you need to crouch so that you can rise with explosive power. This phase of a trick is called *compressing*.

Some moves look best when the skater arches his or her back, often grabbing a toe or wheel. This is called tweaking the body.

Wall Ride—Regular

This description uses a right turn leading into the wall ride. Remember, when attempting this move (as well as all the moves described in this book), always use caution as your guide.

1. Approach a wall at an angle, turning rightward. Extend your right leg and turn in that direction.

2. Compress, while gliding at an angle approaching the wall.

3. Jump and land with both feet on the wall.

4. Ride for a few feet, curving downward.

5. Jump off, leading with your right foot. Skate away.

Wall Ride—Fakie

It's best to use a quarter-pipe for this.

1. For the fakie move, approach the wall at an almost perpendicular angle.

2. Ride up the quarter-pipe. Bend your knees.

3. Ride straight up the wall, with one foot in front of the other (it doesn't matter which foot leads).

4. On the way back down, keep one foot behind you, to feel out the curve of the quarter-pipe.

5. Land facing backwards and skate away!

This trick can also be done on a wall without a quarter-pipe. Use a similar approach, but jump and twist your

*Taking stairs
the fast way.*

*This skater takes the
opposite approach
to the steps that
Rocky made famous.
You only get one
brain — better not to
risk it, especially
when doing a move
like this.*

body in order to ride the wall. Likewise, to land you'll need to jump off with a body twist.

Stair Riding

Stair riding, as you can imagine, can be dangerous. As with all streetstyle and extreme moves, **wear full protective gear**. On the up-side, it can give a great thrill to the street skater.

Look for stairs that offer low, vertical rises and long, flat, horizontal steps. This will make your downward movement less abrupt, giving you a little more control.

1. Approach the stairs frontwards. Extend your lead foot, bend your legs, and lean on your back wheels. Crouch low.

2. Go down the steps, letting your legs do the job. Your legs should bounce with what you hit. Your skates should hit the level part and the corners. Keep your arms extended out for balance.

3. Hit the bottom and ride out.

Backward Variation Stair Riding

This variation is regarded by many street skaters as more fun and actually easier than forward stair riding.

1. Approach the steps backwards in a deep crouch.

2. Place one leg behind you and lean on your front toes (the ones farthest away from the approaching step). Your back foot is now your leading foot—it's a "feeler," sensing for the arrival of the actual drop of the first step.

3. Look straight down as you encounter the first and following steps.

4. Hit the bottom and ride out.

Take pride in your slide.

Rail Slide

Wear full protection before trying these moves, including all standard protection, a helmet with full forehead and back of neck protection, and hip pads.

Novices should practice on a waxed curb before taking on an actual railing. You literally take out a candle and rub its wax onto the curb! Once you've mastered curb sliding, you may decide you're ready for the real thing.

Look for a handrailing that will fit the gaps between your second and third wheels or at least give you a rounded, smooth surface to ride on. Identify your landing area in advance. Also try to choose a rail that's not adjacent to steps, unless you're ready to add a stair-riding combination. In this description, assume the rail is on your left as you approach.

1. Approach the rail from the side, building speed.

2. Compress and jump up to the rail.

3. Land with both feet straddling the railing between your second and third wheels and slide about 8 to 10 feet.

4. Twist your upper body in the direction you intend to land.

5. Land with knees bent and arms extended, and skate away!

At the beginning, try to use a railing with a moderate incline and with grass alongside it. The grass will help soften your fall. Straight rails are much better in the beginning than anything with kinks or curves. (Many advanced street skaters look for "kinky" rails—the stranger the curves, the more fun.) Make sure that the railing will allow you to ride on your chassis (the gap between your second and third wheels).

You need smaller wheels for this move—between 40 and 60 mm, such as are used on some skateboards. With smaller wheels, you'll find it easier to slide on the rail or on your skates' chassis. Harder urethane will provide the least amount of friction as the second and third wheels literally hit the railing. (Some skaters use a metal or plastic grind plate between their second and third wheels.)

Grabbin' air.

1. Approach the rail slowly. Depending on your preference, come at it straight on or at an angle. Righties, for example, often prefer to approach the rail from the right, leading with their right foot.

2. Extend your arms to the side, compress, and jump.

3. Land with both feet on the rail, perpendicular to it. Keep your knees bent. Your arms should be

extended to the sides, with one arm more toward the front and one more toward the back.

4. Jump off by sliding right off, twisting slightly to a forward-facing position, and rolling away. Or add a further twist and land fakie. Yet another variation: spin off 270 degrees and end up facing straight ahead.

You can jump off to the left or right of the rail. Beginners should jump off onto grass to the side of the railing.

VERT AND RAMP TRICKS

Many vert tricks have elements in common. Some vert moves overlap with streetstyle and extreme skating. Because it's all a matter of definition and definitions can be subjective, it's best not to worry much about what classification a trick falls under. Just do it!

Vertical tricks may be done in a pool or bowl or on a ramp. Ramps include quarter-pipes, half-pipes, launch ramps, vertical walls, and fun boxes. A fun box is a structure built for executing tricks and fun moves in streetstyle skating demos. It can include a mini-ramp and various types of coping (piping used at corner edges of

Up-close and personal—Invert at the NISS Competition in California.

ramps). This book contains plans for building your own awesome collection of ramps (see Chapter 13).

Many of the tricks you'll discover in this chapter use the coping, also called the lip. Skaters ride up to the lip, over it, along it, and down it.

Some tricks are described as frontside or backside. *Frontside* means that your chest faces the upward direction as you skate up. *Backside* moves involve your back in the upward direction. *Fakie* refers to riding back down an incline the way you came up—in other words, rather than turning around at the top of an incline, you simply go back down backwards.

Inclines are divided into sections:

- *Flat*—the horizontal area, such as at the bottom of a half-pipe
- *Transition*—the slanted portion of the incline
- *Vert*—the pure vertical rising area
- *Landing or roll-out deck*—the flat upper area beyond the lip or coping

Grabs and Spins

Just about all vertical tricks can be described by their combinations of various grabs, spins, and, in some cases, plants. Briefly described, these moves are as follows:

- Grabs include lien, mute, and stale
- Spins include 180s, 360s, 720s, and even 900s! The numbers refer to the degrees of rotation in a turn done in midair. Of course, 360 degrees constitutes a full turn. Some skaters would say that 180s should not be counted as true spins since they're a common air—going up the transition and vert, turning, and dropping in frontwards.
- A plant or an invert in in-line skating refers to extending your arm onto the coping and inverting or twisting your body.

Grind or Slappy Grind

Grinds have been perfected by skateboarders, who literally "grind" along on the coping by riding their axles. Axles are impossible to ride on with in-line skates—but not to worry! You can ride on the gap between your second and third wheels, using the rail or frame as your riding edge. This move is made in an arcing loop, as you ride up, across the coping, and back down:

1. Ride and compress.
2. Head toward the coping, turning frontside. Keep your arms extended forward and slightly to your side.
3. Position your right skate with your toes pointing upward, across the coping. You're sliding on the rail between your second and third wheels. Your back foot trails along on the vertical surface, perpendicular to the coping.
4. Turn downward and drop back in.

Soul Grind (Vert Version)

1. Ride up the transition.
2. Turn frontside.
3. Arrive at the coping with your feet pointing up in the air (away from the transition).
4. Grind your front foot between the second and third wheels, perpendicular to the coping. Glide your back foot parallel to and along the coping, pointed toward your other skate. The coping should actually rest on the chassis of one side of your trailing skate. The wheels of that skate should hang over the coping, pointing down toward the transition.
5. Drop back in.

Frontside Grind

1. Ride up the transition.
2. Turn frontside.
3. Ride with your feet perpendicular to the coping, with your toes pointing up in the air (away from the transition). Ride with both skates on the rail between your second and third wheels.
4. Drop back in.

Great move — and beautiful hair, but...
Q: What's wrong with this picture?

Chassis Ride

1. Ride up the transition.
2. Turn frontside.
3. Ride with your legs spread apart and pointed in opposite directions, on your rails (on the chassis—not on the gap between your wheels). Your wheels should be hanging over the coping.
4. Drop back in.

AIRS

Airs can be street or vert moves. The point of "getting air" is to soar! As a street move, you can fly over any number of objects. If flying over something solid is your goal, begin with something that'll give way when you hit it. A cone or pylon is a good example.

Street skaters like to get air over any number of obstacles—that's the liberation of it all. Examples? Curbs, for starters. Then boxes, fire hydrants, and whatever comes along. In the movie *The Hoax*, for example, skaters fly over a bike rack.

Do what you're truly *ready* to do—make sure you can do it safely over nothing but air before you fly over any hard realities. And always wear full protective gear.

Anywhere Sports Productions

Aerial freedom.

Mute Air

1. Ride up the transition.
2. Launch into your 180 and begin to grab at about 90 degrees into the turn.
3. Grab across the front side of your body, typically reaching across and below your knees with your hand to the opposite foot. You grab at your instep.
4. Release your grab and land facing frontwards.

Stale Japan Air

1. Ride up the transition.
2. Launch into your 180 and begin to grab at about 90 degrees into the turn.
3. Grab behind and below your body, with one hand grabbing your opposite foot, typically on the heel. Personal preference determines which foot you grab. Extend your un-grabbed foot forward. The direction of your turn can vary, and you can experiment.
4. Release your grab and land frontward.

Gumby Air

During this move you're so flexed backwards, you look like a clay Gumby!

1. Ride up the transition.
2. Launch into your 180 and begin to grab at about 90 degrees into the turn.

© Ari Rosenthal

After mastering curbs, some skaters move on to bigger things!

3. Each hand reaches behind your body and grabs the nearest instep from the inside—right hand over the right ankle and grabbing the right instep from the inside side; left doing same with the left the left side. Grab behind and below your body, with each hand grabbing the opposite foot, typically on the heel.

4. Fully tweak your body, turning your head to the side. The more contorted your body, the better the move! Turning directions can also vary.

5. Release your grab and land frontward.

Lien Air

1. Ride up the transition.

2. Launch into your 180 and begin to grab at about 90 degrees into the turn.

3. Grab your same-side heel at the back of the foot, at the heel or above the ankle. Your un-grabbed foot should mimic the position of the grabbed foot. Position both legs side-by-side and bend at the knees.

4. Release your grab and land frontward.

Judo Air

1. Ride up the transition.

2. Launch into your 180 and begin to grab at about 90 degrees into the turn.

3. Reach behind your body and grab your opposite heel.

4. Extend your leg, as if in a judo kick.

5. Release your grab and land frontward.

Anywhere Sports Productions

The judges say: "10 for form and style!"

Rocket Air

1. Ride up the transition.
2. Turn frontside.
3. Grab your toes with one hand, keeping legs together. Turn your legs 180 degrees as you prepare to drop back in.
4. Drop in.

Cross-Rocket Air

Same as previously, but cross your legs and grab both toes with one hand!

360-, 540-, 720-, and 900-Degree Airs

All of these airs involve spins or various rotations while flying. The more extreme the spin, the more speed you'll need from the flat through the transition and the vert.

Speed alone is not the whole deal. You'll also need extra spring from thrusting off the coping. This gives you more momentum, air, and torque.

1. Ride up the transition. The more spins you want to do, the faster you should ride.
2. Bend at the knees.
3. Launch by pushing off the coping then twist your entire body in the direction you want to spin. Keep your arms close to your body.

4. Spin the desired number of turns. Add any grab you like, including stale Japan, lien, mute, judo, and rocket.
5. Release your grab and land frontward or fakie, depending on the amount of spin you've done as you approach landing.

PLANTS AND INVERTS

Handstands are more common than inverts. Handstands use two hands on the ground or coping; inverts use one.

Handstands

1. Ride up the transition.
2. Turn and grab the coping with both hands on your way up. Flair your knees and your feet above your head, keeping them together and extended straight up.
3. Let your legs fall back in.
4. Drop back in fakie.

Inverts

All of the grabs described in the preceding airs section are invert variations. In effect, you're doing a 180, but you're not flying—you're twisting and letting your legs fly over and behind you. BE CAREFUL!

Anywhere Sports Productions

1. Ride up the transition.
2. Turn and grab the coping on your way up. Your legs will fly out behind and above you. Make the grab you want.
3. Drop back in.

A WORD ABOUT STYLE

Being able to simply attempt or do the moves in this chapter can be quite an accomplishment. But the most talented streetstyle and vert skaters aren't admired just because they can do a particular move.

They also bring their special artistry to what they do. Part of what makes a skater great is creativity. This may be expressed in how the moves are done — body position, height gained, obstacles ridden or flown over, wheels and axles used, and more.

Some skaters involved in extreme skating also have an extreme attitude. Extreme skating includes rail slides, stair riding, and other moves. You can be extreme and creative, if you want to — but having an in-your-face attitude doesn't help anybody. Arrogance in skating doesn't do much for the sport or its reputation. Skate with style . . . and make 'em smile!

Smile for the camera—a one-handed invert.

My In-Line Skating
Tricks and Moves Mastery Chart

(✔)TRICK

❑ Stopping on a slowing surface

❑ Heel stop

❑ Turning to a stop

❑ T-stop

❑ Snowplow

❑ Power stop or hockey stop

❑ Glide turn

❑ Crossover turn

❑ Gliding tuck-style downhill

❑ Criss-crossing hills

❑ Heading uphill

❑ Rock 'n' roll

❑ Hourglassing frontward

❑ Hourglassing backward

❑ Skating on toes

❑ Daffy

❑ Curb jump

❑ Wall riding

❑ Rail slide

❑ Grind or slappy grind

❑ Stair riding

❑ Backward variation stair riding

❑ Soul grind

❑ Frontside grind

❑ Chassis ride

❑ Wall ride—regular

❑ Wall ride—fakie

❑ Mute air

❑ Stale Japan air

❑ Gumby air

❑ Lien air

❑ Judo air

❑ 360-degree air

❑ 540-degree air

❑ 720-degree air

❑ 900-degree air

❑ Rocket air

❑ Cross-rocket air

❑ Invert

❑ Handstand

It's also important to note that the tricks we describe here are only the *very beginning* of what can be done. With experience, you'll be inventing some moves yourself!

AN EXTRA NOTE OF CAUTION

The more difficult tricks described in this chapter require a high level of proficiency. It's best to get the help of someone knowledgeable, who can give you personalized instruction. Always wear full protective gear. For moves this difficult, gear should include hip pads and special helmets that protect the forehead and back of the neck.

Wearing protective gear does not guarentee you won't have an injury.

Track your mastery of different in-line tricks and moves. As soon as you feel you've mastered a trick, check it off!

8

JOIN OR START A SKATING CLUB!

*O*ne of the best ways to enjoy skating is to do it in a group. Skating clubs get people together, teach skills, encourage safety, and—most importantly—create long-lasting friendships. Skating becomes *synergistic* —everyone's energy builds on everyone else's.

This chapter will show you why joining or starting a club is a good idea and will provide suggestions for starting or improving a club. As a case in point, we'll be looking at the Landskaters Club, which encompasses skaters in the southern New Jersey and Philadelphia region. It provides a good model for participation, growth, positive energy, and loads of fun!

LOGICAL FIRST STEPS

Your first step in becoming aligned with a club is to see what's available in your area. There's no point in reinventing even the in-line wheel. Check the newspapers for event listings. Contact skating retailers and find out who's doing what. If you can't find a local group that satisfies your needs, consider starting one.

Contacting National Groups

National skating organizations offer a great deal of support in helping you get started. Call, write, or fax for their full information kits. See Appendix A for helpful information.

Affiliation with IISA, USAC/RS, and NIHA

IISA and USAC/RS concentrate on all forms of in-line skating. Each group offers event guidelines, training programs, insurance for skaters and for club events, and a great deal more. USAC/RS also helps traditional quad skaters. NIHA (National In-Line Hockey Association) is devoted to promotion and development of in-line hockey. If you and your friends are mainly interested in roller hockey, NIHA is a great place to begin.

You may find that a local retailer will pay for your membership in a national organization. That was the experience of Landskaters Club, a group I'll be telling you about in this chapter. A local shop, Danziesen & Quigley, paid for Landskaters membership in IISA. Out of the ten requests the club made of the retailer, this was high on the club's priority list.

Your club may choose to affiliate or go it alone. Either way, it's an option worth exploring, especially as you develop special interests among your skaters. People will need more guidance, and the large organizations give you the benefit of other skaters' experience.

National associations also help skaters with such issues and interests as protective gear, organization of races, and specialized training in in-line hockey, racing, and artistic skating.

Staying Focused on Skating

The Landskaters Club began in the fall of 1992 with a scant six members. Now the club boasts 325 paid members. There are several thousand skaters in the area they serve, which includes parts of New Jersey, Pennsylvania, and Delaware.

Such success has drawn attention from people around the nation. Doug Kelly of the club says that he tries to keep would-be club starters focused on what's important: "Someone might say to me, 'We're in Florida, and skating is rampant here—how can I start a club?'

"I tell them not to forget that the common glue is skating. So at the beginning, eliminate sponsorship and politics. You can deal with that later. Pick a time and place and say, 'Come skate here at 7 P.M. at the old church.' Keep doing that and you wind up networking yourself.

"The people who come out are the ones who help you make the club. Establish the social side of it first. Worry about club guidelines later. It's the skating camaraderie that counts first."

Having people fill out a membership form or setting up a special telephone number comes only after activities and friendships are developed.

By deciding to form a club, you and your nucleus group create a common focus. You're empowered and psyched to spread the word about skating! The feeling becomes contagious. Groups like Landskaters keep the focus on maintaining that energy, especially when unrelated ventures are proposed (as they will be).

"If it's not about skating, we decline," says Kelly. "For example, someone suggested a boat party! Rent a yacht, and have a beer party. It doesn't work! Not everyone is into it. Everyone *is* into skating. It has to be combined with that."

HOW TO START

As people begin joining your informal club, start looking for people who can help out with sophisticated and demanding tasks. Look at members' occupations—discover helpful skills and access to machinery or talent. Don't do it because you're a snob, but because you want the sport to grow and be more fun for everyone!

Case in point: Maybe someone is giving you a hard time about skating near his property, and he complains to officials. The law may be unclear about where and how you can skate. But you discover that a skater in your group is an attorney and can help you get a positive regulation passed by the local city government.

A health-care worker can help your club by giving first-aid training—or perhaps by preparing an article on treating road rash (scrapes from falls) to be handed out to your members. When you tap into people's skills, you get them thoroughly involved in the sport and you help cement friendships. Remember how easy it is to get a group going:

- Set a time and place.
- Run a group skate or offer a clinic.
- Talk it up.
- If you do it, they will come!

Develop a Route—But Be Prepared to Shift

It's important to develop a regular route for your group—a similar path that people skate once a week, based on what city government and local retailers let you do.

According to Doug Kelly, you've got to expect some

© Ari Rosenthal

Skaters rolling down Philadelphia's Ben Franklin Parkway.

grief from somebody—even from politicians. It happened in the City of Brotherly Love, as Kelly relates:

"If someone says 'Don't stop in front of our store,' we change the route. We used to stop at Independence Park. It was part of our route, very scenic, and the bathrooms and benches helped. But we were breaking the law! A ranger told us, 'You can't skate here, this is a federal park.'

"A law had been passed banning in-line skaters from federal park property. So we just changed the tour route!"

Not one to let matters rest at that, Kelly wrote a letter to the National Park Commission. He soon spoke with a high-level official who claimed to be explaining things by saying, "It's a national law."

Of course, mining and hunting on federal property

remain perfectly legal despite their cost to the taxpayer and the environment. The lesson for skaters here is: To the organized goes the power.

Your club may be lucky enough to attract some dedicated people with the skill and passion to fight this kind of stupidity up and down the bureaucratic corridor.

BECOME MORE OFFICIAL

Now you're at the next level. People know your group. Your skate sessions are regularly held and consistently well attended.

At this point, you will notice people in your group saying, "Maybe we should start putting this down in writing and call ourselves something. Let's start a club before someone else does!" That talk grows. Your group adopts a name. Still, you have no business meetings, but there's lots of time to discuss ideas during your regular skate sessions.

When you're done skating and while you're skating, you talk about this stuff. Some come out for exercise and some for the business of the club, too. But you're all activists—concerned about where the sport is going in your area.

Affiliating with Retailers

Now it's time to get the institutional support you need to reach an even wider audience. Your best bet—local retail-ers. Find out who the biggest, most visionary players are in your local in-line retailing market. Approach those people with a list of your top ten needs, your wish list.

The Landskaters decided to feature a few inflated goals, to make the important ones more likely to happen. "Our top requests were bogus items," Doug Kelly readily admits. "We didn't have any money, so we asked them to pay for layout and design and printing of a newsletter, printing of it for a year, printing of membership cards and business cards. Also, we asked them to front us the first portion of the money we'd need to print our T-shirts. Once we got the money back in membership fees, we'd pay the store back."

The deal worked. Among the requests the club had the spunk to ask for were a van, a computer system, and a fax line. Some wishes came true, others didn't. But as you may have noticed, it didn't hurt to ask.

Because Landskaters wanted to be the main source for skaters, one of the requests was for donated T-shirts that advertised the club, not a retailer's name. Many members felt that only the club name ought to go on the T-shirt. Their reasoning was that several retailers had participated in the club's growth, and allowing only one retailer to get exclusive attention would depress support from else-where. A concession: placing the major retailer's name on the newsletter. This kept the T-shirts generic.

What worked for Landskaters may not be right for your group. You may find that a retailer will encourage your club to name itself after his or her store. This way, of course, the retailer benefits from exposure. Your club benefits, too. As you and the retailer grow closer, it will make more business sense for the store owner to invest in supporting your group.

No matter how your club decides to deal with commercial issues, the important thing is to stick to the goal: Help the sport grow. If your goal is the same as the retailers'—to expand the sport, improve it, and educate—everyone benefits. The social aspect of the club tends to draw the people retailers want: serious skating enthusiasts.

Unlike pure roller hockey clubs, recreational in-line skaters' groups tend to be broad-ranging and adventurous. Recreational skaters like to try new gadgets like reflective belts and fanny packs. From a retailer's perspective, that means they're likely to be buyers. In contrast, members of a club that exclusively plays hockey tend to buy just their initial equipment and stay to themselves except for purchasing sticks and balls. Help your local retailers understand these distinctions, and they'll be more forthcoming with support.

A plus for hockey clubs is that their branch of in-line skating is growing at the most explosive pace. This will interest retailers who cater to the in-line hockey crowd and who can sniff sales in the wind!

Clinics

One way to boost your club's growth and, at the same time, contribute to the community is to hold clinics. These are teaching sessions, conducted to elevate the general skill levels of local skaters. In the area where Landskaters was established, a local store was already holding weekly clinics. The club encouraged people to go there to learn. Today, many original club members who attended those clinics have themselves become instructors.

The clinics held by Landskaters follow IISA format. A Beginner's Clinic teaches stopping, turning, striding, and skating. Advanced classes teach advanced braking and turning. Clinics also cover approaching curbs and going up and over curbs and road obstacles; one-on-one instruction on how to go off launch ramps is offered as well.

Skate Patrols

A skate patrol is an event that your club can sponsor to boost attention and interest in your area. The patrol is run by a group of experienced skaters who lead people from one stop to the next on an outing. Patrol members set standards and demonstrate their experience as they assist skaters along a preset route. They also encourage safety by wearing protective equipment.

If you plan a skate patrol, design and circulate a skate patrol fact sheet with a time, place name, and date on it. "Sell" the event with graphics and all of the benefits attendees will get—with the accent on fun!

Have one member of your skate patrol at the front of the group, one at the end, one in the middle, and one sweeping along the outside. The goals are to keep people moving along and to help anyone having trouble. Don't let any skater drop too far behind—those who don't keep up feel uneasy and alienated.

Each skate should have different legs. The point of dividing the skate into legs is to give people a chance to catch their breath at a series of stopping points. Also, because quicker skaters move to the front, this pause allows slower skaters to catch up. And while the slowest skaters are catching up, better skaters can do something other than striding and gliding. Lots of trick skating and socializing happens at the break. If it doesn't happen naturally at first, *make* it happen! People will get into the spirit of the moment and have a ball.

© Art Rosenthal

Weekly Sunday skate organized by Landskaters departs from the Art Museum in Philadelphia.

Contests and Demos

The Landskaters members ambitiously organized their first Philadelphia Demo and Competition. Their event and methods are worth emulating. They worked with the Philadelphia Bulldogs (the region's professional in-line hockey team) and Philadelphia Youth Hockey to show the youth in local hockey leagues that there is more to skating than just hockey.

Not everyone can have a pro team to work with. But you can still build a good event with local stand-out skaters or celebrities. Before its event, Landskaters put the word out and got twenty of the area's best skaters, including people from the Poconos, New York, and New Jersey. The competition included three categories:

- Ramp—judged on freestyle basis

- Cones—like slalom but based on originality and degree of difficulty

- Height and distance—high jump and long jump

The event was organized into team contests and demonstrations. Club members made up the contest as they went along, which was a big part of the fun. After all, why rely on a rule book or printed guidelines for everything?

The club took input from twenty stunt skaters. "Vert and specialty skaters usually have attitudes," Doug Kelly explains. "We stripped them of likes and dislikes for each other, and formed them into teams. We took the best long jump skater, and the best high skater and cones skater, and best freestyle person and separated them—this made the teams even."

Some of those in the Demo were pros or semipros, but no one was paid. All participants got the same thing—just a moment of notoriety before an in-line hockey game, with a box suite for all on the team. This boosted the club's camaraderie. At the end of the Competition and Demo, the winning team was introduced and photographed. All got T-shirts and skate bags and a chance to skate at the Spectrum.

As we mentioned, the event helped draw out non-hockey players. In turn, this gave support to the Bulldogs. As part of a young, growing sport, professional in-line hockey teams are often eager to join in exciting promotional plans.

Fund-Raisers

According to Doug Kelly, holding a fund-raiser to support a club can be fun and a success. "We did a fund-raiser for my wife's speed-skating club at a rink," he explains. "We had over a hundred people come to Echelon Skating Center for four hours. We rented it out, people came and skated in the winter. We made money for the skate team by charging $5 per person. Three dollars in proceeds went to the Omni Skate Club, and $2 went to the rink. The money went to pay room cost at the national competition.

"The recreational skaters took a break and watched the speed club do the same rink at 20 m.p.h. The racers got to see the street skaters do spins and flips, plus jumping. It was a great event!"

Computer System and Mailing Lists

One of the initial founders of Landskaters donated a computer to the club. It's used for mailings and to keep track of when membership renewal is due. Of course, a computer can be helpful in a variety of other ways—producing a newsletter,

answering inquiries, generating flyers, tracking funds, and more.

Newsletters

A newsletter can be a great way to keep your club going, publicize events, attract more sponsors, get people excited, and attract new members. A smart way of beginning is to get local talent involved, as the Landskaters Club did. Members submit articles to a volunteer editor,

As the Landskaters Inline Skate Club knows, club newsletters can help keep your group growing. Note company sponsorship, which helps offset costs.

Courtesy of Landskaters Inline Skate Club

who, when not skating, works for a local advertising agency. The layout person is also a skater!

The Landskaters newsletter goes out to a list of 350 people, including members and nonpaying contacts. It goes to club members who live as far away as San Francisco. Other clubs around the nation get copies, including groups in Utah, Boston, and Connecticut.

TAP INTO THE TREMENDOUS SOCIAL ASPECTS OF SKATING

For many people, exercise is a way of life. With the recognition that exercise and socializing go together, clubs naturally form. The social aspect of skating is very important and tremendously underrated. One good reason for singles to get involved with local clubs is to meet other skaters. According to Doug Kelly, about 80–90 percent of people are in it for the social aspect. Instead of going to bars or dancing, people want to skate together.

Physical sports tend to break down the barriers between people. According to Kelly, "You have this goofy protective gear, and you're sweating and stinking. So what really comes through is people's personalities and their zest, and their traits. Looks and appearance become less important."

But not too unimportant! "Skaters tend to be attractive, because they're into physical culture," Kelly concedes. "They tend to eat better. And skating brings them together. For the same reasons that men bond with men,

because they play football together, skating allows my wife and me to reach another level of our relationship."

The membership of Landskaters is about 75 percent single. Marrieds tend to skate as couples. Very few people skate alone. Husbands and wives skating together appreciate the fact that it's a sport both men and women enjoy. For many couples, that makes it a better choice than tennis or racquetball or football or baseball. This is a great couples sport!

Kelly now personally knows twelve couples who have met through skating, including two who will soon be married. Kelly's neighbor used to skate with the club. However, the club was so successful for him that he has since dropped out—but not out of skating. He met his wife at the club, and now they both skate together.

Families with kids have also recently started going out with the club. As word of the group's spirit and events became public, kids and families started to come out.

There's no guarantee of romance, or even of friendship, in forming a club. But your chances for encountering both are greater than when skating solo. What's more, you'll learn new skills, find new places to skate, and maybe add a beautiful dimension to your life. If that sounds like a sales pitch, it is. Go clubbin' and see for yourself!

9

FITNESS, HEALTH, AND CROSS TRAINING

*I*n-line skating gives your body a great workout. You can enjoy skating for fitness:

- As a break from other sports
- As an off-season way to stay in shape
- As a fitness-focused activity unto itself

This chapter will show you how to stay trim, improve your health, maintain muscle tone, build strength, and understand the important differences between aerobic and anaerobic activities. You'll also learn how to warm up and how to integrate in-line skating with your other recreational activities.

STAYING TRIM

Dietitians, physicians, and sports enthusiasts all recognize that reaching or maintaining an ideal weight cannot be achieved through dieting alone. Effective weight-management plans must also include regular exercise regimes. As you probably know by now, in-line skating is an exhilarating and fun form of exercise.

Who Should Be Interested in Calories Burned?

Everyone is familiar with calories. Calories give us a convenient way of measuring energy expended, which plays a role in fitness conditioning. Calories also play a role in weight management and cardiovascular health. Your physician may recommend that you burn a certain number of calories per day in physical exercise.

However, calorie counts by themselves have little meaning. For example, in any given activity, heavier people burn calories faster than thinner people. The number of calories you burn *should* always be seen in terms of your own body weight and your overall intake of fats and other foods.

In-Line: An Ideal Way to Burn Fat

If you want to lose weight, in-line skating will help keep you in shape. You can expect to burn between 8 and 10 calories per minute, or 480 to 600 calories per hour. Performance skaters can burn even more.

The number of calories you burn by skating varies according to your body and the nature of your workout. Mathematically, it's simple. The total number of calories you burn (work done) in a given activity is the result of calories burned per mile multiplied by the miles traveled.

Calories Burned During In-Line Skating

To see approximately how many calories you will burn in a skating workout, find your body weight in the chart following. Multiply the number of calories you burn per mile times the number of miles you customarily skate. In most cases it's pretty easy to determine how many miles you log when you skate. Check the distance of your skating route by driving a car along a nearby road and watching your odometer (trip meter).

In-Line Skating Compared to Other Activities

Moderately paced in-line skating and running burn calories at approximately the same rate. In-line skating can outstrip stair-stepping in providing an aerobic benefit. This was discovered in a 1994 study commissioned by Rollerblade Inc. and conducted by the University of Massachusetts Exercise Science Department. Ten men and ten women were studied to compare exercise values of various activities. The study found that a 150-pound skater uses approximately 360 calories during a workout of half an hour, when moving at a typical speed. This

CALORIES YOU'LL BURN

Your Body Weight (lbs.)	Calories Burned per Mile	X Miles Skated		Total Calories Burned
100	44	× _____	=	_____
110	48	× _____	=	_____
120	52	× _____	=	_____
130	57	× _____	=	_____
140	61	× _____	=	_____
150	66	× _____	=	_____
160	70	× _____	=	_____
170	75	× _____	=	_____
180	79	× _____	=	_____
190	83	× _____	=	_____
200	87	× _____	=	_____

Data courtesy of Dr. Tony Verde, Graduate Hospital's Sports Medicine Center, Wayne, Pennsylvania.

calorie burn is relatively high. More important, perhaps, is that great speed need not be achieved to get a benefit.

According to Patty Freedson, exercise physiologist and assistant professor at the university, "The study showed that you don't need to be a speed skater. Recreational in-line skaters can travel at safe and comfortable speeds and still obtain a caloric burn similar to running."

Miles per Hour

You may want to compare your speed with that of other skaters. Bear in mind that the right speed for your development will probably be different from somebody else's.

Below is a rough guide to speeds achieved on flat ground by others.

Fat Loss, Dieting, and Those Tempting Fatty Foods

Sure, in-line skating is a great way to burn up fat. But keep sight of your total fat and caloric intake. The story is simple—if you want to lose weight, you must consume fewer calories than needed to maintain your weight. No

FIND YOUR PACE!

Type of Pace	Speed
Casual pace	7–10 m.p.h.
Steady pace	11–13 m.p.h.
Intense pace	14–20 m.p.h.
Race pace	20 + m.p.h.
Championship pace	32 m.p.h.*

*Jennifer Rodriguez achieved this speed on in-line skates. She won three gold medals at the 1993 World Speed Championships. (Source: *Sports Illustrated for Kids*, April 1994.)

aerobic sport in *itself* will be the magic bullet that trims your waistline. Chances are good, though, that you already know that in-line skating does not give you a license to pig out.

Technically, it doesn't matter which exercise you use to expend calories. Take less in, and burn more— you create a deficit. Remember that 1 pound of fat is the equivalent of 3,500 calories. Eat 500 calories less than you need to maintain your weight, and you'll lose a pound a week. That's a reasonable goal for most people.

As an example, let's imagine that you're overweight but neither gaining nor losing weight. If you start expending 500 extra calories a day in exercise, then you will lose weight without adjusting your diet (though it may still need alterations for nutritional and health reasons).

However, exercise is not an excuse to eat more. You might think, "I'm going to have this 500-calorie dessert, but what the heck? I'm going to go out for a skate after dinner, and I'll burn it off." Think again! Is it reasonable to assume you'll skate long enough to work it off and still lose weight for the week?

Enjoy a Fat-Burning Activity, and You'll Do It More

Okay, so I've gotten your hand out of the pantry and now you're bummed. Cheer up—here's the good news.

In-line skating is fun! *Fun* matters for medical reasons, simply because it keeps you "on the program." Major in-line manufacturers well understand how important the pleasure principle is to in-liners.

"Our studies show that most people skate because it is so much fun," says Noel Shadko, vice president of marketing and strategic planning for Rollerblade Inc., in a Rollerblade news release. He adds, "A fun workout is one people will stick with over time."

If you choose to commute by skates, you can carry your good shoes or dress clothes in a knapsack.

Skating to Work and at Work

Is skating just a weekend activity? Not if you don't want it to be. In cities all around the world, people are skating to and from work.

If you choose to commute by skates, you can carry your good shoes or dress clothes in a knapsack.

The Lunch-Hour Roll

You can also try in-lining at lunchtime. Here's how to organize a lunch hour for maximum rolling:

11:45 A.M.–noon: Enjoy a yogurt and an apple or another easy-to-eat meal at your desk, while you work. Computer users can crunch a byte while munching a bite.

Noon–12:10: Jump into skates and safety gear. Change clothes if necessary.

12:10–12:45: Skate like a mad person!

12:45–1 P.M.: Cool down, change clothes, and hit the bathroom to wash up. No shower? No sweat: use a sponge and splash on some cologne or perfume.

At a few advanced work sites, showers make it easy to thoroughly freshen up before returning to work. Of course, those who work at home can fit in a quick shower easily.

Do you give up something by choosing to skate at lunchtime? Not necessarily. For instance, you don't have to give up socializing—not if you persuade friends and coworkers to take up the sport and join you.

Skate at work, and you'll skate during sunny hours. That's an important consideration. Think about it: Getting sunlight matters. Psychologically, sunlight improves our moods and elevates our beta-endorphin and serotonin levels. In winter, lunch-time skating gives you a benefit you can't get at another time of day. Think of how unlikely you are to skate at night in winter. What are your chances of wanting to jump into skates at 7 P.M., after you've had your dinner? Here's what will happen: You'll be feeling full. You'll look outside, see it's pitch black, and say "forget it."

So don't forget it! Skate at work, and you'll skate often.

Hidden Skating Benefit: Increase Your Metabolism

Regular aerobic activity, like in-lining at a taxing speed, will give a small but significant boost to your metabolism rate throughout the day. So you'll get a calorie-burning lift even when you're not skating.

According to Dr. Tony Verde of Graduate Hospital's Sports Medicine Center in Wayne, Pennsylvania, "There is a residual increase in metabolism after exercise, during the recovery portion, that's based on the exercise bout, the duration, its intensity, and the fitness level of the individual. In other words, if you're in really good shape, you recover quicker. However, metabolism in general is elevated compared to a person with a higher fat proportion.

"Even sitting in a chair, a fit person burns more calories. Lean muscle tissue burns more calories than fat, which is an inert tissue."

Achieve Heightened Body Awareness

By working your body hard (if that is your goal), you will become more aware of how you feel and look. Your greater awareness will probably help motivate you to avoid overindulging in fattening foods. In addition, once you've become more trim and in better physical condition, you'll find it easier to stay that way by continuing to skate!

HEALTH BENEFITS FROM IN-LINE SKATING

Exercise does more than burn calories. Its overall beneficial effects on the body are immeasurable. The health benefits of skating regularly—as with any regular, sustained physical activity—include decreased cholesterol, lowered blood pressure, weight control, reduction in the likelihood of obesity, stress reduction, resistance to cancer, and improved bone density.

The Cardiovascular Benefit

In the past few years, physicians and cardiologists have focused increasingly on the cardiovascular benefits of exercise. Their thinking has changed in a few important ways: Intensity and length of exercise time are not considered as important as they once were. In other words, people who go from being couch potatoes to being regularly active can achieve a major cardiovascular health benefit.

According to the earlier school of thought, achieving a certain heartbeat rate for a certain number of minutes at a certain frequency was required to achieve a cardiovascular benefit. The official position of the American College of Sports Medicine regarding recommendations on exercise and lifestyle habits holds that risk factors for cardiac incidence are reduced by staying active—not by being an extremist in exercise.

How does this information affect you as a skater? Let's put it into practical terms: Habitual, long-term activity provides a health benefit equal to that obtained by individuals who train with great intensity. If you go out for an occasional skate, starting and stopping, you're getting a cardiovascular health benefit that's not much different from an intense workout.

To be beneficial, your skating should be habitual—10 minutes a day is much better than one 70-minute bout by a weekend warrior. Here's yet another reason to make regular skating a part of your lifestyle!

Your Regular Blood Pressure Benefit

Any regular habit of physical activity will help decrease your blood pressure, but you'll be helped more by aerobic activities in which you move your body around more. If you have blood pressure problems or want to avoid them, your physician's advice should come first.

BUILDING STRENGTH AND STAMINA

Exercise builds muscle. Muscles provide strength. The cardiopulmonary benefits of exercise increase stamina.

The more you exercise, the longer you can work hard—at a sport, a job, or a household task.

Power for Performance: Fitness Buffs and Racers

People who want more stamina—whether for general living, other sports, or skating sports—will benefit from regular *intense* skating. The fitness buff needs to be on a more regular path than the casual skater—he or she needs to push farther and longer.

Aerobic and Anaerobic Exercise Benefits

In evaluating the fitness benefits of in-line skating, it's helpful to know the difference between aerobic and anaerobic activity. An *aerobic* activity is exercise at a rate that allows the body to successfully consume oxygen supplied to all of the working muscles. *Anaerobic activity* is conducted at a rate *beyond* which your body can consume oxygen supplied to all of the working muscles. Anaerobic activity raises the threshold of aerobic activity. In other words, skate intensely and often, and you will be able to skate faster and faster—yet still feel you're at a comfortable pace.

When people think of anaerobic activity, they think of intensity. For instance, power lifting uses high percentages of maximum strength during each repetition. Very intense in-line skating can be anaerobic—for example, sprinting at all-out speed is anaerobic. Muscles build up lactic acid in the blood during anaerobic activity, which you may experience as a rubbery feeling in the used muscle.

Casual skaters should be pleased that skating is *aerobic*—which means it gives cardiovascular and weight-management benefits. In-line racers, on the other hand, need to seek the benefit of anaerobic intense training, which builds endurance and strength. This will help them perform aerobically at higher racing paces. They need to push their anaerobic threshold so that they can work at a higher percentage of their maximum speed and still work aerobically (see Chapter 11 for guidelines for in-line racing training).

Bear in mind that you need to create some serious speed in order to get an anaerobic benefit from skating—in other words, to build yourself up in terms of speed and endurance. Racers need a velodrome or track to do oval or speed work. Even bicycle paths present obstacles that keep racers from achieving high speeds for long periods of time.

The Importance of Regular Exercise

Building a regular workout into your schedule is a great way to be sure of getting into shape. Try to do your workout with somebody you like, who has similar fitness goals. When you have someone to meet, you're more likely to show up and actually complete the activity. Plus, you'll have the pleasure of chatting with your friend during the less intense parts of your workout.

To give you a regular way of improving your conditioning, Rollerblade Inc. has produced a special 10-week workout, which is reprinted here with permission (see chart). This plan was developed as part of the Rollerblade/University of Massachusetts Fitness Study. To receive a free copy of a complete brochure containing this workout and many other fitness and conditioning tips, write to Rollerblade Inc. at the address shown in Appendix A.

Note that the workout mixes different kinds of activities during the same week. Pick a day of the week arbitrarily as "Day 1". For example, if Monday were "Day 1," then Wednesday would be "Day 2" and Friday would be "Day 3," etc. Then follow the instructions on the chart for each numbered day of the week. Where no activities are specified on a given day, you may rest or pursue additional activities.

Use this workout as a guide, but always remember to skate at a pace you find personally comfortable.

ROLLERBLADE ROLL & TONE 10-WEEK WORKOUT

Week 1	**Rolling Around**
Days 1, 2, and 3	Familiarize yourself with your skates. Practice speed control, braking, and turning skills.
Course:	Find an open flat area, free of cars, bikes, and people and practice skating for 20 minutes.

Week 2	**Get Rolling**
Days 1, 2, and 3	Map out a safe, open area and get rolling. Skate in steady strides. Remember to exercise in moderation—build endurance before tackling a more difficult level.

Course:	3 miles
Complete in:	20 minutes
Calories burned:	144
Average speed:	9 m.p.h.

Week 3	**Loop It**
Days 1, 2, and 3	Add an extra loop to your route, increasing the length of your course, but still complete it in 20 minutes.
Course:	3.5 miles
Complete in:	20 minutes
Calories burned:	176
Average speed:	10 m.p.h.

Roll & Tone workout courtesy of Rollerblade Inc. and University of Massachusetts Exercise Science Department.

ROLLERBLADE ROLL & TONE 10-WEEK WORKOUT (CONTINUED)

Weeks 4–6	Interval Training
Days 1 and 3	Alternate your course by mixing longer segments of steady skating with shorter intervals of fast skating.
Course:	5 miles
Complete in:	30 minutes
Calories burned:	264
Average speed:	10 m.p.h.

Weeks 4–6	Mix It Up
Day 2	Today, shorten your course and time, but continue mixing quick sprints with long glides.
Course:	4 miles
Complete in:	20 minutes
Calories burned:	208
Average speed:	4–11 m.p.h.

Weeks 7–9	Advanced Interval Traning
Days 1 and 3	Increase your speed and course length by following the same interval program as the last 3 weeks, but skating faster overall.
Course:	5 miles
Complete in:	30 minutes
Calories burned:	264
Average speed:	10 m.p.h.

Weeks 7–9	Short and Steady
Day 2	Shorten your course and skate steadily, using constant strokes and glides.
Course:	4 miles
Complete in:	20 minutes
Calories burned:	238
Average speed:	4–12 m.p.h.

Week 10	Top-Notch Training
Days 1 and 3	Go even faster to build your endurance. Increase your speed and distance.
Course:	7 miles
Complete in:	40 minutes
Calories burned:	352
Average speed:	10 m.p.h.

Week 10	Short and Steady
Day 2	Skate quick and fast, incorporating smooth, long strokes and glides.
Course:	4 miles
Complete in:	20 minutes
Calories burned:	238
Average speed:	4–12 m.p.h.

Total calories burned over 10 weeks: 6,408

Note: Calories burned are estimated for a 150-pound person. To adjust for differences in weight, add or subtract 0.6 calories for every 10 pounds you weigh above or below 150 pounds.

CROSS TRAINING

Because in-line skating uses so many muscle groups and because the basic skating motions resemble those of other sports, it is excellent for cross training. Cross training

may be viewed as a *parallel* activity that uses the same or similar motions as another sport. For example, ice skating and aspects of skiing use similar motions.

Integrating Skating with Other Sports You Enjoy

In-line skating may be regarded as an alternative activity that *complements* another sport. For example, skating can be an excellent alternative sport for weight lifters. Without an aerobic activity such as skating or jogging, weight lifters' routines are often incomplete.

You might want to consider in-line skating as a cross-training activity. The discussion that follows describes how skating compares to other sports and gives tips for using it as an alternative activity, when appropriate.

- *Running and jogging.* Joggers' knees often take a pounding. In-line skating gives the knees a break. The caloric difference between running and skating is small—the calorie expenditure for skating is about 7 to 10 percent lower than that for running. If you want the same fitness benefit you get when running, cover more miles during your skating workout.

- *Skiing.* Both alpine and cross-country skiers will quickly spot similarities between their sports and in-line skating. Alpine skiers will find that skating helps develop muscles of the thighs and buttocks. In slalom work, techniques are nearly identical between in-line skating and downhill skiing.

Many balancing and turning moves are similar as well. Cross-country skiers may even want to use their poles during skating workouts, to better simulate Nordic stroking techniques and balancing.

- *Ice skating.* In-line skating was *invented* as a warm-weather alternative to ice skating. Both employ the same muscles, including those of the thighs, buttocks, and groin. At a roller-skating rink, you can work on the same techniques that you'll use in ice skating for taking turns and straight runs. Whether your ice-skating goal is sprinting, high-speed endurance, or freestyle tricks, you will find parallel training moves on in-line skates.

- *Using a treadmill or stair machine.* Machine-tended workouts are fine for staying in one place, but in-line skating gives you a pleasant change of pace! Keep in mind, however, that these machines are available at your gym or club when the weather turns brutal.

- *Biking.* In-line skating will improve your leg strength, especially if you skate up steep hills. High-speed skate racing—both sprints and marathons—will improve your cycling ability in those respective areas.

- *Swimming.* Although swimming gives you a better upper-body workout than skating does, in-lining lets you take great advantage of a beautiful day!

- *Skateboarding.* Though skateboarders need to be

agile, strong and knowledgeable, the number of calories they burn is small in comparison to those burned by skaters. Also, some skating—such as sprinting—can be anaerobic or strength-building. Very few skateboarders use the sport to build strength.

Warm-Up Exercises

To reduce your chances of injury, warm up before an intense skate. This will allow your muscles to become more flexible before they are subject to the stress of a workout (see page 50 for warm-up exercises).

Goals: Strength, Speed, and Endurance

The best way to achieve fitness and skating skills is to work closely with a trainer or coach who can help you to establish a training program to match your goals.

You'll find it helpful to understand some of the basic concepts underlying your fitness training. The following measurements of performance are all interrelated, and each has a different set of training guidelines for numbers of repetitions and types of exercises to be done.

- *Endurance*—Relates, for example, to the ability to compete in an in-line marathon
- *Power*—Work over time or during a time period
- *Peak strength*—Most important to sprinters
- *Speed*—Important to sprinters

A skater stretches before the Pro Women's 500-meter sprint.

If you intend to remain a recreational skater, you need not be concerned with all of these qualities—except insofar as you want to be stronger or skate faster. But keep in mind that strength helps prevent injury. The stronger your muscles, the less strain on your joints during peak exertion. In addition, scientists are now discovering that the contractile force around bone and the weight-bearing aspect of the activity both help increase bone density.

In other words, *muscle building makes for stronger bones.* For example, swimming is not a weight-bearing activity and is not helpful in preventing bone loss. In-line skating, on the other hand, is weight-bearing. Women, who are in greater danger of osteoporosis as they age, should be especially careful to choose weight-bearing activities.

We all lose bone density to some degree as we age. Most people have insufficient calcium intake and exercise too infrequently to keep their bone density high. Skating can be part of the answer to this problem for all of us.

Strength training for in-line skaters applies most directly to racers. They need to develop most of their lower body muscles, such as thighs, buttocks, groin, and calf. Most of the strain of skate racing is on the upper thigh. Running is more of a lower leg sport.

Competitive skaters, such as racers, need to develop their back muscles also because they're bent over a great deal. The back muscles do not do the work of the stroke but rather help maintain the posture of the upper body.

A strength-training tip: If you want to race faster, you may wish to use lower durometer wheels (70s) for more resistance and leg-muscle strengthening during practice. The extra resistance makes you stride harder.

Hand Weights

Some skaters use hand weights, but they can interfere with your ability to catch yourself in a fall. Hand and wrist injuries are the most common accidents suffered by skaters.

Ankle Weights

You can use light weights—a pound or a half-pound—around the ankles. These put a little bit of drag on the legs and can help build strength. A more efficient method of building leg strength is to skate harder or head uphill. If you do use ankle weights, be sure you can maintain your balance!

MEDICAL PROBLEMS AND SKATING

Most of the medical problems associated with skating can be prevented by using proper equipment and following the basic health rules that apply to participation in any sport.

Skating When You Have a Cold

According to Dr. Tony Verde, a moderate workout during a light cold probably won't hurt you. If you feel psyched for a skate, go for it. It may speed up your recovery. Moderate exercise enhances your immune function. Intense exercise impedes it.

On the other hand, if your energy level is poor, why bother skating? When you have a fever or an infection, don't skate. Your fever will probably break within 24 hours anyway.

Treating Road Rash

Use common sense in treating injuries that result from a fall. If you break the skin, clean thoroughly and apply hydrogen peroxide. Any accident more serious than a scrape, cut, or minor bruise demands medical attention.

Dealing with Sore Muscles

You can't do anything about feeling achy. Once your muscles are sore, just stretch and work through it. You've created some slight tissue damage—just *kvetch* (Yiddish for "gripe"), and go out and do it again!

If you tear a ligament or damage a joint, the pain will be severe. You'll know you need to see a doctor. Always put ice on an injury or swelling. When you remove the ice, you'll magnify the blood flow to the area. This increased blood flow speeds the healing process. More detailed guidelines on treating a soft tissue injury can be found in the next section.

Massaging aching muscles can feel good. Liniments have no healing physiological action, but they can make you feel good. However, going for a walk may be just as effective!

Treating Injuries with RICE

If you have an injury which you suspect may be serious, see a physician immediately. The following suggestions are for relatively minor injuries, such as ankle twists. Review the advice contained in this section with your physician before you begin any self-treatment.

For minor soft tissue injuries, the recommended treatment is RICE, which stands for Rest, Ice, Compression, and Elevation. You may also wish to use a mild painkiller and anti-inflammatory agent, such as ibuprofen.

First, rest. Get off your feet.

Second, apply ice. You can do this with an ice pack or with a plastic bag full of ice cubes. If you like, shield your skin from close contact with the cubes by wrapping a towel around your ice bag. Cold reduces inflammation and minor bleeding. It also chills nerve endings and reduces muscle spasms.

Apply the ice for 20 minutes or so per hour, for about 48 hours. Be sure to avoid frostbite! Use common sense, and remove the ice pack when you feel your injured area becoming too cold.

Compress the injured area by wrapping it with an elastic bandage. You can accomplish two goals at once by wrapping the ice pack and the injured limb with one bandage.

Elevate your injured area, keeping it raised higher than your heart. For example, sit back on a sofa with your leg elevated on pillows atop a chair.

Finally, consider applying heat, but only after 48 hours. Do this on the third day after your injury. DO NOT apply heat if the injured area is either inflamed, infected, or sensitive. If applying heat makes you feel worse in any way, stop immediately. In such cases, heat will only make the situation deteriorate.

You may alternate four minutes of heat treatment and one minute of cold treatment now, using warm and cold water or other sources of heat and cold. During the warm phase, gently exercise your injured limb.

Dehydration/Loss of Electrolytes

On hot days, you may overheat faster than you realize—and faster than your body can adjust. As a result, you may become dehydrated quickly, even on days that aren't scorchers. Any time you sweat profusely, you are likely to suffer from dehydration. You can lose your body salts and become weak or even faint.

Dehydration can leave you vulnerable to the more serious heat exhaustion and heat stroke. It's wise to carry a water bottle—especially on hot days. Drink a couple of cups of water for every pound of sweat you lose. You'll find that in cooler weather, you need not drink as much.

Weigh yourself before and after you skate. If you lose more than 2 percent of your body weight, you may be susceptible to problems. If you go out for a long skate, bring water.

trolyte replacement as part of your fluid intake. Examples include Gatorade, Cytomax, or other so-called sports drinks. Cytomax is sold in many bike stores. Taking salt tablets after intense sweating is no longer recommended.

Some skating routes actually feature drinking fountains. For example, Central Park has a drinking fountain near Central Park South. In Philadelphia, Fairmount Park's Kelly Drive offers at least two free water spots. Know where your reliable watering hole is, and you may be able to skate without the encumbrance of a water bottle.

Heat Cramps

Any muscle cramp can be a heat cramp. It feels as if you've pulled a muscle. The cramp is a sign that your muscle has become dehydrated. It's also a reflection of your total body dehydration.

How do you avoid heat cramps? Drink a little now and then while you skate. Get water from a bottle you keep in a fanny pack or from a fountain. If you consistently take in water all along, fluid loss should not be a limiting factor.

A hint: drink *before* you get thirsty. You might not feel thirsty, even though you're losing a lot of water through sweating.

Heat Exhaustion

In general, you need be concerned about drinking fluids containing electrolytes only if you're a racer or if you skate more than an hour at a time. If so, consider an elec-

When heat exhaustion hits, you will feel it as nausea, weakness, and dizziness. It's brought on by sweating at a high rate—several liters per hour. Heat exhaustion often happens when people start skating in the summertime in great heat.

Warning signals vary: If you don't cramp, you may instead feel yourself getting weak. Competitive athletes push themselves through these signs. This is a bad idea and may lead to the more serious heat stroke.

In heat exhaustion, the body's core temperature goes up, though not higher than 104 degrees. Your blood pools in your arms and legs. You may feel rubbery or notice an actual pumping up of the muscles.

When you start feeling heat exhaustion:

- Stop exercising.
- Move to a cooler environment.
- Drink liquids.

If you're in a race and these steps don't help, go to a medical tent to get 5 percent glucose or another solution administered through an IV.

Heat Stroke

Heat stroke—a failure of your heat-regulating mechanism, associated with body temperatures above 104 degrees Fahrenheit—is the most serious heat-related disorder and requires immediate medical attention. Your blood is fighting so hard to dissipate the heat that you can tax your heart.

Get medical help before you suffer heat stroke. Noticing and responding to signs of heat exhaustion is the key to avoiding heat stroke. Listen to your body when you notice heat exhaustion symptoms, and slow down or stop skating entirely.

Hypothermia

Cold-weather skaters need to take special care to avoid becoming seriously chilled. Your body will usually manufacture enough heat, even during cold weather, to compensate for the heat you lose to the elements. But on a long skate in a bitter wind, where little shelter is available, hypothermia (too little body heat) can be a problem. Help guard against this by not skating too far from your car or another warm place during very cold weather.

Also consider wearing extra layers of clothing, and carrying a knapsack in case you want to shed them. If you develop more body heat as you move along, then just put the excess clothing in your knapsack.

In general, you can hardly find a more enjoyable way to stay fit than by in-line skating. Do it outdoors, and you have scenery to enjoy. Indoors, you're free from weather worries as you zip along.

Having fun is what it's all about, both now and when you get older. The activity you like is the one that's going to help you get fit—and stay that way.

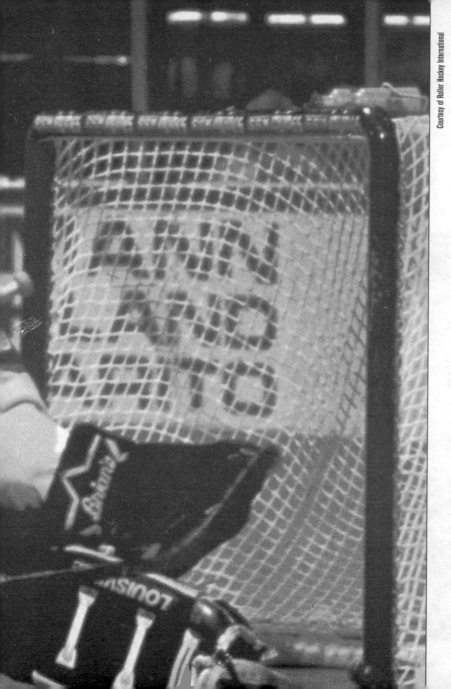

10

IN-LINE HOCKEY

*R*oller hockey delivers a rush—the adrenaline that only a fast-moving team sport can deliver. It's a great way to channel your skating skills into another pleasurable direction.

In this chapter you'll learn about the sport's origins, organizations, equipment, and rules; you'll also learn how to play and how to form your own team and more.

HOW ROLLER HOCKEY BEGAN

Ice hockey came first, then quad-style roller hockey, and, finally, in-line hockey. The four-wheeled versions of the sport gave ice hockey players a way to stay sharp—even in July! Many National Hockey League players train with in-line skates in the off season.

AMATEUR IN-LINE HOCKEY

The fast-moving, intense sport of in-line hockey (or roller hockey) has gained tremendous popularity. According to *The Philadelphia Inquirer* (June 8, 1994), there are more than 25,000 amateur teams around the country and almost 800,000 players. The National

Fast hockey action stokes the blood!

In-Line Hockey Association (NIHA) places the figure much higher—at 1,500,000 players in 1992. They project growth to 7,500,000 by 1996. According to one important sports industry source, American Sports Data, in-line hockey is now the fastest-growing sport in the United States.

In fact, roller hockey is bringing more new participants to in-line skating than is racing, dancing, vertical tricks, extreme skating, or anything else.

In-line hockey is an especially strong sport in the United States and Canada. Although 70 percent of participants are youths, adult leagues are now being formed in many locales.

Courtesy of Roller Hockey International

The National In-Line Hockey Association

The National In Line Hockey Association (NIHA) helps popularize the sport in the United States and Canada. The Miami-based group is the main organizational body for in-line hockey and is supported by many groups and companies. It is the logical place to start if you are considering forming a club or a league or are looking for support and affiliation for your club. See Appendix A for address and telephone number.

Courtesy of Roller Hockey International

NIHA was formed in July 1992 by Joseph Mireault to guide the sport and help it grow. The group is an independent organization that standardizes rules and regulations and helps people manage leagues all over the United States and Canada. Organizations as well as individuals may join.

NIHA will organize a National Championship in the fall of 1995. State and regional competitions take place in the summer and fall, leading up to the nationals.

NIHA-sanctioned games can be played almost any-where—and often are. Of course, teenagers will put a puck in motion on just about any place with a flat surface. NIHA has established rink standards (discussed later in this chapter). Typical sites for league games include parking lots, asphalt basketball courts, rinks, and indoor gyms. Games take place in all fifty states, plus Puerto Rico.

The group offers a comprehensive insurance program. The policy's coverage includes player excess accident and league general liability insurance, fire legal liability, and referee and skate rental insurance. League managers, property/facility owners, and sponsors may all be added as additional insureds under the policy.

The NIHA Official Rulebook covers many subjects, including rink diagrams and dimensions, protective gear, pucks and balls, game time, the game team composition, penalties, age recommendations, referee's signals, a glossary, and more. An instructional video has also been produced.

The organization also offers a hockey coaches' certification program through The National Youth Sports Coaches Association (NYSCA). Administrative software is also available.

To help retailers promote and expand the sport, NIHA provides the Preferred Retailer membership. This program costs $200 per retailer and includes a listing on the NIHA database, a store promotional package, a retailer guidebook, access to retail insurance, and other services and benefits.

NIHA is now expanding into Canada—a natural direction, since 12,000,000 Canadians already play ice hockey.

Plans for future programs include development of grass roots leagues; coordination with parks and recreation departments across the country; cooperation with schools, the military, and civic organizations; stronger relations with ice hockey groups; and development of women's hockey.

IISA and In-Line Hockey

The IISA, or International In-Line Skating Association, also helps develop the sport at the amateur level. Both NIHA and IISA develop guidelines and can help direct you to a local club or league (see Appendix A).

IISA promotes the sport, sanctions leagues, and offers insurance programs and a comprehensive *In-Line Roller Hockey Guidebook*.

USAC/RS and In-Line Hockey

The United States Amateur Confederation of Roller Skating (USAC/RS) sanctions leagues and offers rulebooks for all of the divisions of hockey it supports. The group sanctions many local events but hosts national competitions, which are held in different cities in the United States every year. USAC/RS has a coaches' program and offers insurance.

USAC/RS has been involved in roller hockey on quad skates since its inception in 1937. National championships in ball roller hockey were first held in 1961, and those for puck roller hockey in 1962. Championships have been held every year since then. Now USAC/RS supports five types of roller hockey, all of which climax in championships:

- *Ball hockey.* Played with a hard ball, which is made of hard rubber(the same substance hockey pucks are made of).

- *Puck hockey.* Just like ice hockey.

- *Standard softball.* Nothing like the popular sport played on ballfields across the country. This version is roller hockey but played with a softer ball than the tough hard ball that is used in ball hockey.

- *North American-style roller hockey.* A game played with a long stick and a softball.

- *Junior Olympics.* Held in four age categories. The game is played with short sticks and softballs. This program is for beginners in their first three years of competition. Players may graduate to any of the other divisions after participating at this level.

A sixth form of the sport, called USA Roller Hockey, will be organized in 1995. USAC/RS will be sanctioning local leagues in what it terms a grass roots roller hockey program—no national championships will be held.

Skating equipment in all USAC/RS divisions remains the skater's choice, with most participants now using in-lines.

PRO ROLLER HOCKEY TAKES OFF!

Two professional in-line hockey organizations recently joined forces: Roller Hockey International (RHI) and the World Roller Hockey League (WRHL). The upshot is the RHI league, which formed in 1993, fielding 12 professional teams. In 1994, the league doubled to 24 teams and even has a contract with ESPN and ESPN2.

The pro game features four 12-minute quarters with no ties. Field size is larger than that for amateurs but the same as the professional ice hockey players use: 200 feet

Courtesy of Roller Hockey International

by 85 feet, all on a synthetic surface. Teams are made up of five players.

Each team will play 22 games from early June through mid-August. Teams include (check out these colorful names!) the Philadelphia Bulldogs, New Jersey Rockin' Rollers, Florida Hammerheads, St. Louis Vipers, Atlanta Fire Ants, Minnesota Arctic Blast, San Diego Barracudas, San Jose Rhinos, Sacramento River Rats, and Vancouver Voodoo.

The sport is expected to grow quickly. After all, more kids play roller hockey than ice hockey these days, and they're bound to provide future players and current fans.

Many pros are ice hockey players who need only a few weeks of adjusting to the differences of in-line before being able to play the roller game at a high skill level. The most important elements in roller hockey are hockey sense and stick-handling ability. Special in-line skills are a distant third consideration. Hitting and checking happen often in pro games, but fighting isn't allowed.

HOW ROLLER HOCKEY DIFFERS FROM ICE HOCKEY

Besides having only five players instead of six and not allowing body checking, playing hockey on asphalt feels different from playing on ice. For street players, there's more to fall on—gravel, oil, dust, sand, dirt, leaves, and twigs. Stopping is a lot harder—you can't use your edges the way you can in ice skating. Roller hockey skates have no heel stops.

Even pros have their problems at first. Listen to Steve "Bogie" Bogoyevac, player and captain for the Los Angeles Blades RHI team: "In my first scrimmage, I must have fallen a dozen times," Bogie told *Sports Illustrated for Kids* (July 1994). "I kept trying hockey stops, and boom! I'd fly over the boards."

Stopping is basically done by dragging a foot behind you (T-stopping) or turning. Turning is just as easy on in-line skates as on ice skates.

THE RINK

Rink size is typically 180 feet by 80 feet for amateur groups. NIHA rules permit rinks as large as 200 feet by 100 feet, down to 145 feet by 65 feet. Professional in-line hockey teams play on a 200-foot-long rink. Amateurs play two 22-minute halves, with a 5-minute break between halves. Pros take the rink for four 12-minute quarters.

One of the challenges in keeping a roller hockey game fun and fast-moving is to keep the puck from continually flying out of bounds. An organization called In-Line Sports Systems appears to have licked the problem. It makes a foam-pad border that can help reduce the frustration of pucks and balls flying out of bounds. The system comprises fifty foam boards that strap together. Each is vinyl-covered, 10 feet long and only 7 pounds in weight.

According to the company, setup is quick and simple, with four people needing only 15 minutes to assemble a

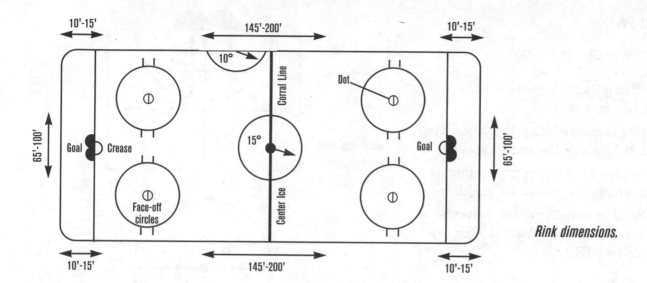

Rink dimensions.

180-foot by 90-foot NHL-type rink (see Appendix C for more details).

WHERE TO PLAY OUTDOORS

Chances are good that you don't have a space specifically built for in-line hockey in your neighborhood. But don't let that stop you. Good spots abound. Get creative.

One of the best places to play may be a tennis court. The asphalt is probably ultra-smooth. Use two halves of two courts to avoid the net area. There will be a fence on at least two sides of your impromptu rink, helping trap out-of-bound shots. Other possibilities include basketball courts, parking lots, seldom-used streets, and driveways. Avoid busy streets! It's hard to watch traffic and play at the same time.

PLAYERS AND POSITIONS

Both amateur and pro in-line hockey teams field five players: a goalie, left wing, left defender, right wing, and right defender. In-line pro teams can have up to fourteen players on the team, even though only five may play at any one time.

RULES AND HOW TO PLAY

These are the basic rules of in-line hockey:

1. There must be five players: a goalkeeper, two defenders, and two forwards.

2. No body checking is allowed. Legal violence has been banned to help widen the sport's appeal.

3. A player may receive a pass from any teammate at any location — there are no offside penalties.

4. The game is played in two 22-minute halves. (Some groups use 15-minute halves, though this is not sanctioned by NIHA.)

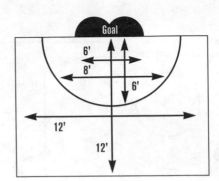

Goal and goal crease.

PARTS OF THE RINK

The parts of the rink include *goals*, *circles*, and the *crease*.

Goals should measure 72 inches between goalposts and 48 inches from the surface of the rink to the top of the net.

There are five circles on a rink — a *center circle* and four *face-off circles*. Each circle is approximately 10 feet in diameter with a dot, approximately 1½ to 2 feet in diameter, in the center.

The very first face-off is held at the center circle, where a referee drops the puck. If you have no ref, you can just have the puck in place and appoint a bystander to count to three to initiate play.

After a stoppage of play, such as when a player falls

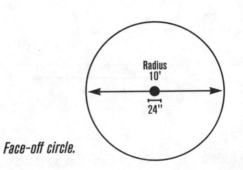

Face-off circle.

on a puck or after a penalty, the play resumes in a face-off circle nearest to where the stoppage occurred. Each face-off circle has "hash marks" indicated.

The crease is the goalie's privileged area in which no other players are allowed. It extends 12 feet from the mouth of the goal and 12 feet from either side of the center of the goal. If a player enters the crease, the ref will stop play.

The goalie is allowed to go as far as center ice, but he can only stop the puck in the area between his goal and the closest hash marks. If the goalie freezes the puck in any manner—such as covering it with his gloves—beyond either of the closest hash marks, a delay of game will be called.

Note: Additional clarification of dimensions, rules, signals, and other aspects of the sport can be found in *The NIHA Official Rulebook*. See Appendix A for information on contacting NIHA.

HOCKEY EQUIPMENT

With all of the banging and scraping that goes on in roller hockey, the equipment needs to be much more durable than that made for normal in-line skating.

Boots are tougher and stiffer. If you expect to be playing roller hockey more than skating in the street, get in-line skates built especially for hockey. These are made by Bauer, Rollerblade, and many other manufacturers.

Gear made for hockey must be extra tough, flexible, and breathable.

Protective Gear

Banging is common in roller hockey, so bulk up with protective gear—especially if you're in a competitive league and especially if you're a goalie.

Goalies need padded gloves, a helmet with a face mask or guard, chest and arm pads, extra-heavy-duty shin guards, waffle pad or board, catching glove, and (guys only!) a jock with a protector cup.

What do the other players need? Everything! Your chances of taking a spill or a hit in hockey are far greater than in street skating. Wear all protective gear, including a helmet and wrist, knee, and elbow protectors.

Sticks

Three basic considerations—weight, length, and composition—come into play when you're choosing the right stick.

Choose a weight that you can heft comfortably and swing with force. In a sporting goods shop, find a bit of open space, make sure no bystanders are in the way, and swing away.

Children should choose shorter sticks that they can handle easily. Bigger kids, teenagers, and adults will want the longer models.

You have six basic choices in the composition of your stick:

- *All wood.* Advantage: more flexible. Disadvantages: more likely to splinter and fracture at the blade, which requires a new stick. Warps with moisture.
- *Wood and plastic.* Advantage: easy to replace the plastic blade.
- *All plastic.* Advantages: more durable than wood if you don't smash it. Won't warp in rain. Disadvantage: a break in the blade requires a new stick.
- *Aluminum.* Advantage: practically impossible to break. Disadvantages: can chip and can develop sharp edges. Once cut down, it can't be extended with a longer shaft.
- *All graphite.* Advantages: doesn't chip easily, very durable. Lightweight and strong. Disadvantages: chips a bit. Slippery in beginning. Vibrates with hits, so you need to get used to it. Requires flexing before a game.
- *Aluminum shaft and graphite blade.* Advantages: could be the best stick for most people. Light in weight, durable, easy to replace parts.

Beginners, especially kids, should get an all-wood stick. They probably won't break it. Kids 8–10 should get wood and plastic, because this combination won't break easily and is highly durable. The correct choice for everyone else depends on personal preference.

Blades and sticks come in right-handed and left-handed models. On a right-handed hockey stick, the concave side should be facing forward when you're in wrist shot position.

Pucks and Balls

A roller hockey puck is lighter than an ice puck (3 ounces versus 6 ounces)—it also travels faster and rolls on its side more easily. Pucks come in many varieties, including:

- *JOFA SpeedPuck.* The official puck of Roller Hockey International, as well as of USAC/RS and many amateur groups. However, the National In-Line Hockey Association (NIHA) makes no specifications about the type of puck or ball that may be used in competitions by its affiliated teams and leagues.

- *Standard roller puck*. Three or four bearings embedded in the bottom. Advantages: on a smooth surface, it travels faster than a ball. Unlike a ball, it will take a direct hit without flying over the blade. Disadvantages: bounces a lot and rolls on its side too much. Also, if this type of puck gets wet, the bearings will get rusty and make the puck useless.

- *Puck with Velcro bottom*. Advantages: won't slide up a goalie's waffle glove and into the goal. Velcro slows down the puck, enabling more accurate passing. Disadvantages: rolls on its side a lot. Collects grass and dirt on the Velcro surface.

Buying tip: Rubber pucks tend to last longer than plastic ones in outdoor play, because they can better withstand freezing and thawing.

Pucks are no longer the universal choice in roller hockey. Balls are preferred by many players. A street hockey ball is made of hollow rubber or plastic. Most don't bounce much. Advantages: easier to stop; won't roll over the top of a blade easily. Easier than a puck to pass; easier to see if you're a goalie. Doesn't hurt as much if you get hit.

Goals

Prefabricated goals may be bought in most sporting goods stores. The goals come in different sizes and types. Some are made of tubular metal: 3 feet high by 3 feet wide (for small children); 4 feet high by 6 feet long (NHL size, for bigger kids and adults). Avoid non-regulation-sized goals, unless your car will have problems transporting a full-sized goal to games.

ROLLER HOCKEY MOVES

Try to master all of the basic moves described in this chapter. They will add to your repertoire of skills and make you a better player.

Stick Handling

Stick handling is the equivalent of dribbling in basketball. It's the way you control the puck while moving. Move the puck back and forth in front of you, in your "control zone," which is the same width as the distance between your shoulders. As you prepare for a shot or pass, move the puck to your forehand or backhand side.

The best way to practice your stick handling is to find some smooth asphalt (or your basement floor) and practice moving, turning, passing, drop passing (passing behind you), and shooting.

An example of good stick (and sister) handling.

Slap Shot

1. Skate up to the puck.
2. Hold the stick with your weak hand on the end of the shaft, and your strong hand two-thirds of the way down toward the blade end.

3. When you're about 5 to 10 feet from the puck, rear the stick back behind and above you.
4. Swing at the puck in one fluid motion. Try to add forward sweep to the puck by keeping your stick motion parallel to the ground for as long as possible before lifting it.

Wrist Shot

1. Skate up to the puck.
2. Hold the stick with your weak hand on the end of the shaft, your strong hand one-third of the way down from the top of the stick.
3. Gain control of the puck on your strong side, behind you.
4. In a sweeping motion close to the asphalt, thrust the puck forward.

Snap Shot

This shot is just like a slap shot, but you bring the stick back only to mid-thigh level. Use this shot when you are so close to the goalie that there is no time to wind up into a full slap shot.

1. Skate up to the puck.
2. Hold the stick with your weak hand on the end of the shaft, your strong hand two-thirds of the way down toward the blade end.

3. About 5 to 10 feet before you reach the puck, rear the stick back behind you to mid-thigh level.

4. Swing at the puck in one fluid motion. Try to add forward sweep to the puck by keeping your stick motion parallel to the ground for as long as possible before lifting it.

Back-Handed Shot

In this version of the wrist shot, you shoot in the direction of your stronger hand. If you're right-handed, shoot rightward; if left-handed, leftward. This uses your weaker arm muscles and usually feels less natural when first attempted. This shot works as a pass or a scoring shot.

1. Gain control of the puck.

2. Put the puck on your backhand (the reverse of the scooping side of the blade), keeping the blade parallel with your feet.

3. Shoot in the direction of your strong hand. Follow through with your body weight for added power, shifting from your weaker to your stronger foot.

Faking

It's important to fake out your opponents so that you can get good scoring opportunities. Faking requires movements of your arms, legs, and head. Practice your abrupt, tricky moves until *nobody* knows what you'll do next!

Passing

Your team may have good stick handlers, but unless you're also good at passing, your team's progress will probably be limited. Remember that passing is a lot faster than stick handling. *Speed* in passing will help you get ahead of the opposition. To the skilled passers go the goals. The following are the basic moves on forward passes:

1. Stick-handle the puck while moving up-rink.

2. Check your teammate's position; gauge his or her direction and speed.

3. Pass, using a low sweeping move. Do not slap the puck. Aim at the spot where you expect your teammate's stick position *will* be.

4. Follow through with your stick kept low to the ground.

Receiving a Pass with Your Stick Blade

In most cases, you'll want to receive a pass with your stick blade on the forehand side.

1. Look for the pass. Yell "Here!" if your teammates don't see you.

2. Keep your legs spread and your blade out in front of you, closer to your dominant foot and low to the ground.

3. Take the pass while moving your blade backward a bit to cushion the impact and reduce the ricochet effect.

Receiving a Pass with Your Skate

When the action comes thick and fast, you'll want to receive a pass with your skate.

1. Keep your weight on your strong foot.
2. Lift your weaker foot, and place it at an angle so that the puck faces the sides of your wheels.
3. Let the puck ricochet off your skate.
4. Gain puck control with your stick.

Sprinting and Skating Backwards

Even a goalie has to sprint occasionally. Getting around fast is often essential, especially when using the breakout strategy (described later in this chapter). You will want to develop your sprinting skills both for offense and for getting back quickly to help on defense. For a detailed description of sprinting technique, see Chapter 11.

When your opponents are on the offense, you will often need to skate backward to keep your eyes on the action (see page 62).

SKILLS AT POSITIONS

Goalies need quick legs and hands and excellent reflexes. The butterfly always proves useful in stopping goals. This is a drop-down move by a goalie, to stop a shot on goal that's aimed low:

1. Drop down to your knees with your shins spread outward and your stick between your legs.
2. Keep your weak hand extended, low and to the side—to give your body extra stopping power.
3. Be prepared to shift left or right quickly, and to jump up if necessary.

Defensemen must have terrific backward-skating skills and a knack for anticipating where their opponents are going. Defensive players also need a good long-distance shot, since they'll often be far from the opponent's goal. Some stars can even shoot from center court and score!

Forwards need to be fast and able to skate forward well. Faking abilities are paramount—they're your ticket to getting yourself past defensemen and the puck past the goalie. A forward needs quick, strong wrists, not powerful arms.

STRATEGIES

Stick handling and shooting are skills you can develop on your own. But hockey is a team game requiring strategies, some of which are outlined in this section. As you and your team develop, you'll add strategies of your own.

Box Strategy

In this defensive strategy, all players except the goalie move in a boxlike pattern in response to their opponents' line of attack. In other words, if opponents come at you

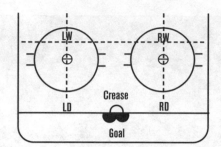

Box strategy.

from the right, the whole group shifts rightward—while maintaining similar positions relative to their teammates. The "box" moves as one. The left and right wings (forwards) never fall farther back than the upper portions of their face-off circles.

Diamond Strategy

The diamond strategy is just like the box, but rotated on its side! Some typical locations for players in this formation could be:

1. Left defenseman in the right-hand portion of his face-off circle

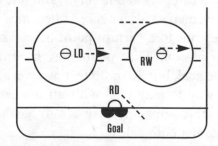

Diamond strategy.

2. Right defenseman in front of the net

3. Right wing moves to the right-hand portion of his face-off circle.

Breakout

A breakout is an offensive strategy that begins in your own half of the rink. The play can begin with any defenseman. Let's assume the play begins on the left side of the rink. The left wing stays on his outer defensive hash marks.

1. If the play begins on the left side of the goal, the left defenseman falls back to left of the crease.

2. He receives a pass from a teammate, or he already has the puck. He looks for an open winger.

3. He gives it to the left winger, who then passes it to the right winger, who is at mid-rink. He looks for a chance to shoot or pass.

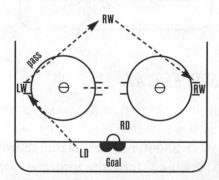

Breakout.

4. The right winger skates up-rink and now receives a pass at about mid-rink.

From there on your success depends on speed, skating, stick handling, and shooting abilities.

God's Country

In the offensive strategy called God's country, your team's prime shooting area is defined by a trapezoid. The trapezoid has as its upper corners the posts of the defender's goal. Imaginary lines extend outward from those posts, passing near the inside part of the face-off dots and continuing outward to the blue line.

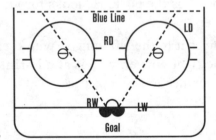

Offensive zone.

INFORMAL STREET PLAY

When playing with your friends, you can have a game with as few as three or two players total—if you have a Shooter Tutor. A Shooter Tutor, manufactured by GDS Sports (see Appendix C for more information), is a plas-

tic sheet that fits over the frame of your goal, kept in place with clasps. It has small openings in the upper and lower corners, as well as in the Five Hole, or center bottom. Use the Shooter Tutor as a constant goalie, so you and your friends can play other positions.

One person can play defenseman, and one a forward. When a defenseman steals a puck, he becomes a forward. He has to step out to a certain point or mark, or a tree that must be passed. That point may be any distance away from the goal, but 20 or 30 feet away is about right.

Another way to play well with an uneven group of players is to have someone play steady goalie (that is, play goalie against both sides).

In a half-court game, you can play in various uneven combinations, including:

5 Players	7 Players
1 steady goalie	1 steady goalie
2 forwards	3 forwards
2 defensemen	3 defensemen

league in your neighborhood. See the extensive list of local hockey clubs in Appendix A. Or call NIHA at the phone number given in Appendix A. You'll be giving yourself a new, enjoyable way to stay fit—and you'll have a great time year-round!

PLAY IN-LINE HOCKEY AND BE A PART OF THE FUN!

Few sports in America are growing at the rate of in-line hockey. You can be part of the excitement. Join a club or

11

SPEED SKATING AND RACING

*O*nce racing gets in your blood, it tends to live there. The urge to go fast—faster than others—can easily become a part of your nature. This impulse to race goes back at least to the Greeks and the ancient marathons. There, the winner of a race was honored with a laurel crown.

Humans have raced not only on foot, but also with horses, bicycles, automobiles, boats, and ice skates, just to name a few variations. The invention

125

of the roller skate brought a whole new way to compete. With the advent of in-line skates, traditional roller skaters quickly and literally lost ground.

Today, in-line skate racing may be pursued as an enjoyable part-time activity or as a dedicated dimension of your life. As a skater, you will reap many benefits from racing:

- Improved fitness and cardiovascular health
- A regular way of having fun on skates
- A sense of accomplishment and mastery as you improve
- An easy way to manage your weight
- A way to enjoy the pleasure of competing—win or lose
- A chance to meet and work with other skaters and enjoy their company
- The opportunity to shine when you win

In this chapter, you will learn about types of races, racing techniques, training strategies, and organizations that support racing.

A question before we start: Is skating or cycling faster? Not long ago, a speed skater and a bicyclist tem-

© Ari Rosenthal

Racers are tightly grouped at the start of a 10K race.

porarily settled the question with their respective wheels.

Sorry, folks. We lost this round! A 100-meter race held in Downers Grove, Illinois, in front of 20,000 spectators, pitted U.S. national cycling champ Steve Hegg against USA World Games speed skating team member Tony Muse. It was close—a photo finish, in fact. Hegg nosed out Muse with a time of 10.55 seconds. Nevertheless, Muse's time was impressive, when you consider that an in-line skater can't change gear ratios the way a cyclist can.

Let's hope for a rematch — after in-line skating takes yet another leap forward in technology.

Meanwhile, in-line speed skating continues to build momentum. Skate manufacturers have been busy popularizing this aspect of the sport. For example, the Geo Rollerblade Racing Team, one of the first and most prominent racing teams, helps promote the sport by racing against new teams being formed. The Geo Rollerblade Team really *moves* — in the 10K, they've averaged an amazing 22 m.p.h.!

IS RACING FOR YOU?

Perhaps you're attracted to racing on its own terms — you love the idea of speed on wheels and competition. Then go for it!

If you're not sure you want to race, consider the many pleasures of the sport. You may discover that you love the competition. In addition, you'll meet new people and possibly develop close friendships with other racers. There's plenty of team spirit among racers, even amidst the individual competitiveness.

If you're a college or high school athlete, once you go out into the working world, you may miss the fun of competing and enjoying sports with your friends. This is a way to keep that great team feeling alive!

Be prepared to spend a great deal of time training if you want to become an accomplished racer. Training can be fun — and exhausting. You'll get aches, pains, and blisters. But with any luck, you won't care — you'll be having too much fun!

Clubs, Teams, Organizations, and Skating

Indoor skating, focused on traditional roller skates, has been around for nearly 50 years and is very well organized. It's much easier to find clubs and teams for indoor racing than for the outdoor version of the sport. The first indoor quad speed-skating national championships took place in 1937. Racing was one of the most popular forms of roller-skating competition. These days, most quad skaters have converted to in-line. Traditional roller skating requires slowing down at corners, which puts the roller skater at a great disadvantage.

Once you get involved, you'll find converts from quad skates as well as long-time in-line racers in your area. A great way to start is to contact a local, recreational in-line skating club. Join or become acquainted with the local members. If you can't find someone locally, contact IISA or USAC/RS. Whether you're interested in indoor or outdoor racing, they'll refer you to the right organization or person in your area.

Although few local clubs have specialized subgroups dedicated to racing, that may change as the sport grows in popularity.

Outdoor competitions on in-line skates have been organized by IISA since 1991. Organizations that were active in the sport in earlier days are now defunct. However, IISA and USAC/RS have brought new enthusiasm to racing, and this aspect of the sport continues to grow at a rapid clip.

Look for a Racing Team and a Teacher

Most outdoor racers have no access to a club with a certified coach who can teach speed skating. Indoor racing clubs, however, often offer clinics and sponsor races. So to learn true racing, you should ideally begin *indoors*, with a certified coach from a team or a club.

If your efforts to find a local club don't pan out, contact your nearest in-line retailer to find out where the in-line racing action takes place in your area. Many local race teams are organized around outdoor racing, with retailers taking a lively interest in sponsoring teams and races.

Remember that each of the major national skating organizations will be able to help you in your search.

SPECIAL EQUIPMENT

General guidance on in-line skating equipment is covered in Chapter 3. This section discusses equipment particular to racing.

Short Uppers

By choosing racing skates, you're sacrificing ankle support for flexibility and light weight. Most racing skates are lace-up only, in soft leather.

© Ari Rosenthal

Zipping in a 10K race.

Custom Boots

Some stock boots are custom molded around the ankle — heat-molded to your foot. The bottom of the boot is made of Kevlar, which can be shaped with a heat gun to meet the contours of your foot.

There is still a lot of experimenting going on to find the right materials and fit for the most comfort. Many racers prefer boots made by Bont, an Australian manufacturer. K2 and Rollerblade are also active in this specialized field.

Don't buy a boot a size and a half bigger or even a half-size bigger than your foot. You want to eliminate friction and give your foot greater control over the rail (chassis). A good fit is a prerequisite for accomplishing both of these objectives.

Close-fitting boots help you skate better and faster. But be careful — if you tie your skates too tightly, you'll get a "pins and needles" sensation and numb legs. Once your skates are too tight, you can't stop racing to loosen them unless you give up all chances of winning.

Helpful hint: Wax your laces, to help make your close-fitting boots stay that way.

Five Wheels

All serious racers skate on five wheels rather than four, for added speed. Anyone attempting to go fast on four wheels may be having fun — but won't be able to race competitively.

Chassis, Rails, or Plates

The chassis is usually made of aluminum, housing and supporting a five-wheeled skate. Almost all quality racing skates come as separate components. The chassis is one of the key separate components that you will purchase.

Dutch brands, such as Viking and Mogema, were among the first specialized in-line racing boots. Viking makes an ice boot that also gained popularity. Mogema is a prominent plate manufacturer and the pioneer in making "rails," now called chassis or frames.

Most elite skaters buy components from various manufacturers. Rollerblade and K2 make complete race packages that come with axles. There are holes in the bottom of a special soft leather racing boot where you position your plate.

It's important that you be able to move your plate. When you're skating indoors, both plates are positioned slightly to the left — because you're going around to the left. When you're skating outdoors, plates on each skate should be positioned under your big toe. If you're shifting from indoor to outdoor, this would mean that you'd shift the plate on your left foot from its indoor position (closer to the little toes) to its outdoor position (below the big toe). Your right skate would not require adjustment.

Fast Bearings

Racers need especially fast bearings, and personal preference comes into play when making a choice. Bearings are often identified by manufacturers as designed for either recreational or speed skating.

Many speed skaters use Swiss Bones bearings. They have a reputation for speed and smoothness, with a light oil. The bearings are serviceable, meaning they're not completely sealed. One side is sealed, and the other has a "crown ring." You can pop out the crown ring and view the bearings. The ball bearings don't fall out, because they're trapped in a small track.

Most bearings come with an extra supply of bearing oil. It might be a year before you have to relubricate your bearings (see the discussion on bearing lubrication on page 42). Rather than use standard oil lubricants, you may wish to use a specialized lubricant for an even faster glide. Your bearings may not last as long, but you need to take every speed-boosting advantage you can get.

Twin-Cam brand bearings have a white gel inside. But heavy oils and gels also attract particles. If you break a seal, you're out of luck! The bearing becomes no good.

A popular cleaning fluid for bearings among racers is carburetor cleaner or brake cleaner—or any degreaser. Most racers prefer a lubricant of very light weight. Some racers use WD-40 or Liquid Wrench to lubricate their bearings. Liquid Wrench is fine for short races such as a 5K, but it dries out. WD-40 or any other thin oil will be better for longer races, such as those of 10K and above.

Bearings preferred by racers include ABEC-1, -3, and -5. But ABEC-5 bearings, while supposedly built for high speed, are very receptive to dirt. Most racers prefer ABEC-1 or ABEC-3. If you don't clean bearings or don't lubricate them, naturally they'll become a problem.

Remember that the bearing doesn't make the skater. As long as you have an ABEC-1 or -3 and it's clean and well-lubricated, you're bearing-equipped.

CLOTHING FOR RACERS

Socks

Thinner socks are better for skaters. Cool-Max brand socks are a double-layered sock, each layer being a blend of cotton and a synthetic fabric. The layers of material wick away moisture to help dry out your feet. Because they have two layers, Cool-Max socks can wrinkle easily; and a small wrinkle can cause a lot of pressure while you skate. So pull your socks on tightly.

Racers use low-cut ankle-length socks—anything to reduce wind resistance. Some men even shave their legs to be more aerodynamic! Shaving the legs also reduces the chances of infection after a case of road rash.

Some excellent skaters wear no socks (scandalous!). In the end, wearing socks is a matter of personal choice.

Tops, Pants, and One-Piece Outfits

Most indoor and outdoor skaters wear a one-piece outfit with a zipper that goes from the crotch to the neck. These are made of Lycra or cotton Spandex or other materials that breathe well. These one-piece outfits end at mid-thigh and have short sleeves. The top is like a T-shirt. Remember that the more skin exposure you have, the more road rash you're open to!

In cool weather, you may want to add a thermal top below your one-piece and Spandex tights on top of the one-piece. Expect the added layers to slow you down. In the winter, your normal 18-minute 10K may become a 23-minute 10K. But you'll still feel as if you're going fast, even considering all of the extra clothing you're wearing!

PROTECTIVE GEAR FOR RACERS

ANSI- and Snell-approved helmets are usually required at indoor races. Outdoor USAC/RS race organizers will also demand the use of ANSI- and Snell-approved models.

Nothing else by way of protective gear is required by race organizers, and most elite indoor and outdoor skaters wear no other protection. But skaters are vulnerable! Racers can fall up to a couple of times per practice. Falls during races are less common, but do happen occasionally—including pile-ups at the corner. If someone goes down and you're drafting behind, you're going to go right down as well.

Wear protective gear, especially if you are a beginner or unsure of your abilities. To protect their knees and elbows, some skaters wear a ¼-inch-thick neoprene pad originally designed for wrestlers. Some racers also wear racing gloves with a small plastic palm plate to help shield you during a fall. The skater's version stops at the wrist.

Lazy Legs and Rollerblade make a brand of these gloves.

Racers have no brakes because of the extra weight they bring. Stopping requires a T-stop or a snowplow. However, a snowplow is very hard on your quadriceps. Most people slow down over a lap or two and then use a T-stop to come to a halt.

FOOT BLISTERS AND HOW TO TREAT THEM

It's very common to get foot blisters when breaking in new boots. The best way to avoid blisters is to get proper-fitting boots.

Many skaters wear a neoprene sleeve around their ankle, which can help prevent a blister from forming. Some people tape their ankles or feet with white medical adhesive tape or even duct tape!

Although "ankle sleeves" as such are not available, you can buy a neoprene ankle brace, which can be formed into a sort of ankle-only sleeve. However, because the full ankle brace covers too much of your foot, you will need to cut off the instep or arch section. This will help avoid friction with the side of your boot.

You may wish to use moleskin, a product sold in drugstores and supermarkets. It's a feltlike substance that can be used over a blister or around it. You can use moleskin to form a protective doughnut-shaped patch. The idea behind this doughnut shape is that it creates a protective ridge around the blister, guarding it from further contact with socks, boots, etc. To make your patch, you begin by cutting a circular piece bigger than the blister. Fold this circle in half. Next, cut out a half-circle the size of the blister. Now apply it to surround the blister.

If you're fortunate, your skin may callus—form a dead skin patch that helps protect you from future blisters. But not everyone will develop this protective mechanism—so protect yourself as well as you can at the beginning.

SPECIAL WATER AND HYDRATION NOTES FOR RACERS

More than most skaters, racers need a regular supply of water flowing to their systems. For general information on dehydration and heat-related ailments, see Chapter 9.

Plan on drinking at least one cup of water every 15 minutes, and more if you're sweating heavily. Also consume fluids containing essential electrolytes, such as Gatorade.

Carry a water bottle, especially on longer practice skates. Manufacturers now produce a water-bottle waist strap that keeps the bottle on your back in a comfortable position. You could also wear a light backpack, which could hold fruit, an extra shirt, and other helpful items (including your shoes!).

When speed skating in competition, where water is banned from the skate floor or track, you drink up beforehand. Plan to drink *before* you get to the check-in or ready area, where water is banned. Once you check in, you can leave for water, but you may miss your race. On a 3,000-meter indoor race (3K), the longest kind of indoor race, no breaks for water are necessary.

On 50K or 100K outdoor races, many skaters have CamelBak packs. You sip from a special long straw that comes with the pack. Race organizers sometimes hand out drinks at a special spot—perhaps on top of a hill, where skaters are going more slowly.

Some racers like to place a water bottle at a particular point on an outdoor track. They'll ask someone to hand it to them while running along nearby, so as to reduce any need to slow down greatly. If you use this method, when you've drunk your water, toss the bottle to the side or share it with other skaters.

TRAINING FOR RACERS

Training typically consists of stretches, work on technique, and exercises. For stretching exercises, see Chapter 6. Your training should be done on an individual basis, with an experienced coach. Different events have different requirements. Your training schedule depends on your goals and the time you have available.

Few people can train nearly full-time. Perhaps only thirty professional in-line racers are making a living at the sport. Many are part of teams like Team Geo Rollerblade, Hyper, Kryptonics, and K2. And these teams are not made up of racers alone—many include nonracers, people who are stunt, dance, and vert skaters.

Even if you can't devote the amount of time to racing that a professional can, you may still be able to reach a very high level of achievement with dedication. To begin, turn to one of the large skating organizations, and find a club and a trainer.

Derek Parra's Training Program

The following program was devised for this book by world-champion speed skater Derek Parra, who skates for Team Geo Rollerblade. This program sets up good, yearlong training goals for outdoor and indoor work. All of the distances given can be done on an indoor track.

Remember that any training program should be customized with your coach to suit your special racing goals. Derek also cautions that he has a bias toward extensive cross training. He enjoys it and finds it helpful, but others will have to find what works best for them.

I. Power Training Phase

The power training phase covers October, November, and December. Put in 30 or 40 miles on the bike. Or

skate long, which comes to about 20 or 30 miles. Add some weight work.

Derek also recommends isometric exercises (stroking and holding the stroke). Now is the time to focus on technique work — the fine points of how you move and how it all comes together.

This is not the time for skating fast — it's the time for slow work. "I do this three times a week," Derek says, "in the winter months from October through January."

II. Speed Training Phase

From January to March, begin accentuating longer distances and more speed. This is the time to work less on power than on rhythm. Spend half your skating time on sprints and the other half on distance. Indoor skaters should do more laps, similar to distances you'll be racing. Taper down your weight work now.

III. Racing Phase

April through August are your months for working on speed — these are usually the prime racing months. Do sprints and intervals, and maintain threshold paces.

"I ride one time a week for 30 miles," Derek adds. "Other times, shorter—such as 15 miles hard. This is the threshold pace—short, hard, and fast. I do 45 minutes a ride, almost as hard as I could without sprinting. I do it on a nearby road.

"There are a lot of Amish people out here, so they have 6-foot road shoulders for buggies. That's great for training!"

Weight Training for Racers

Some top athletes do no weight training, yet others make it a regular part of their regimen. In any case, your goal for your upper body should be to improve tone, not add bulk—you don't want to gain upper body weight. Consult with your coach on weight training and your particular goals.

Special Cross-Training Notes for Racers

Having diversity in your training can help keep you fresh. Racers use a variety of cross-training sports, including bicycling, running, slide boarding, and swimming.

Some top skaters run one day, bicycle another day, and use a slide board a third day. As with weight training, the kind and type of cross training you do depends on your goals, what appeals to you, and the advice of your coach or trainer.

See Derek Parra's thoughts on cross training, in the interview on page 143.

RACING

Most races can be divided into rough phases:

- Starting sprint
- Stroking, turning, drafting, and leading (all part of the middle of the race)
- Passing
- Pacing
- Breaking away
- Finishing sprint

Starting the Race

For indoor racing, begin by getting down in starting position, almost as if in a runner's starting block. Typically, seven to nine skaters are placed on an even line. Most tracks use a regular hardwood floor.

You will hear, "Skaters, to your mark." Then "Set." Then the starting gun.

Expect to move in the starting moments like a foot racer, even though you have wheels. In-line racers use a fast V-walk or a duck walk to sprint. Your arms should swing sideways to help you get traction.

Everyone hits onto each other, until the first left turn, where a pylon or cone is placed. No one should actually be skating (stroking) until that first pylon.

If there is a false start, the race will be halted. The person who commits a false start will be penalized by four feet. After two false starts, a racer is disqualified from the race.

Stroking

A racing stroke involves the following moves:

1. Push out mostly to the side and a little behind you with one leg. Keep your elbows bent and arms close to your body.

2. Lead with your left leg as you enter a turn.

3. Push out with your leg, using your outside edge.

4. Return your foot to the outside edge—almost in a bow-legged position.

At the Olympic level of competition, the fewer strokes made to complete a lap, the better. As few as ten to twelve strokes per lap are standard for a pace that will win a medal. *More stroking tips:*

- *Knees close.* When one leg crosses the other, make sure one knee comes very close to the other.

- *Push out, not back.* You generate forward thrust by pushing outward, to your side, not behind you.

Indoor Inside Crossover Turning

This key move involves three or four crossovers around the corner, before you enter the brief straightaway. Your upper body should be nearly horizontal throughout the turn. To turn:

1. Give one push with the left leg to the side.

2. Give a push with the right leg. This makes you "fall" to your left. The fall is where you build acceleration.

3. Bring your right leg back in and cross over at least 10 inches or as far over as you can. This makes you lean far over on your outside left edge.

4. Use your left leg to push farther to the right for extra speed.

5. Enter the straightaway and you're into the next turn.

Very talented racers need only cross over twice during a turn. Bear in mind that most bursts of speed in indoor racing are generated by the turns.

Drafting

Skaters take advantage of other racers in position before them, who are cutting through the air. Racers moving in a line ride the vacuum they leave behind. This is called drafting. It's more important in outdoor skating, especially on a windy day.

Everybody is always drafting somebody else. When racers lag so far behind that they cannot draft anyone, it almost always means that those racers will not finish among the leaders.

With indoor racing, there is always a pack, inches apart—perhaps just a hand's distance. In outdoor racing, you should place yourself perhaps an arm's distance from the other skaters.

When drafting, stay within the stroke of the person

in front of you to get the most benefit from the draft. If you're out of sync, you're not taking advantage of others' efforts as you should.

The power of the draft is so great that you can be pulled along and almost not stroke at all! This permits you to rest and expend your energy to pass later.

If you practice racing alone, you won't learn drafting. You may build yourself up physically, but you'll miss out on the strategic interaction with other skaters.

Leading

In outdoor racing, it's never preferable to lead. However, you *must* lead sometimes, for ethical reasons. It's your way of sharing the load. Proper etiquette dictates that everyone takes a turn being the leader.

In outdoor racing, there can be one pack or several packs. In men's outdoor racing, the race often breaks up into two or three packs, plus stragglers. In indoor racing, the term "pack" is not used as often, perhaps because there is usually only one group—rather than competing packs. Additionally, indoor races usually involve as few seven people, versus perhaps twenty or more for some outdoor races. Any straggler in an indoor race usually ends up getting lapped. The referee decides whether that person has to move to the outside and get out of the way of the pack—or be disqualified.

Stay with the pack for most of the race, at almost any cost. Remember, if you lose the pack, you'll lose the race.

When racing indoors, especially in 500- or 1,000- meter races, you want to be in the lead. In longer distances, you can let someone else take the lead and work your way to passing them.

Passing

After taking the lead, you need to fall behind and take your place in the pace line. Your teammates will make a space for you by skipping a stride.

Be advised: members of other teams may give you a hard time. You might get your foot kicked by someone's stroke, whether intentional or not. This can send you flying off balance, at perhaps 18 to 20 m.p.h.

If you're racing indoors, there are several kinds of passes you can use:

- *Power Pass*. This is the most common pass. When going into a corner, you drop back and give the skater in front of you a little bit of room—a few feet perhaps. This creates a gap that you can move into. Then you drive hard on your opponent's left and come up just at the completion of the corner (curved part of the track), completing the pass on the following straightaway.

- *Late Pass*. Regarded as a surprise pass, the late pass occurs after an opponent passes the last stroke of a straightaway and is entering the corner. You accomplish this pass by stepping out to the left, moving forward, and immediately hitting your right inside edge as you round the corner.

- *Outside Pass.* As you approach the corner, you take the outside route. You pass one or two skaters to their right on the corner.

- *Outside/Inside Pass.* Here you pass one skater on the right around the corner then another skater on the left on the straightaway. The second phase of this move is the same as the Power Pass.

- *Between-the-Cones Pass.* This is a very sophisticated, but rarely attempted, pass. It occurs around corners when a skater leaves too much room (arc) between the pylons and is passed on the left inside. The passing skater is always to the right of the cone, of course—"between the cones" simply refers to cones at the beginning and the end of the corner.

- *Outdoor Passes.* Here the choices are few: you can go left or right. Just leave a little room for yourself and explode out to the side of an opponent. Many people pass on an uphill. Stronger skaters take advantage of their strength and take other, more fatigued skaters by surprise.

Ultimately, passing locations depend on the individual and the nature of the course. It's usually less important in outdoor passing to time your stroke precisely to the movements of an opponent than it is in indoors.

In a short race, everyone, even teammates, may jostle one another. Each skater wants to win—so be ready. Better yet, surprise them!

Pacing

The first person in a pace line literally "sets the pace." Sometimes another person in the pace line feels that the pace is too slow and will pass the leader. At other times, a pace may be slow but nobody cares. Maybe the track is not superb for creating a new personal time.

Depending on the distance of a race, you may wish to take it slow during the first half, and faster in the second half. You will typically see this pattern in a race that's 10K or longer. By contrast, a 5K race is a sprint from the beginning to the end.

In general, though, you have nothing to do with the pace of the race when you're in the pack. It's beyond your control—except for the moment when you take the lead and in your final sprint.

When pacing, an experienced racer uses no arm movement. It's a good idea, however, for beginners to swing their arms.

Making a Break

With perhaps a couple of kilometers left to go, you may decide to break away from the pack. A breakaway is different from the final sprint, which everybody does. You should decide to make a break based on several factors:

- The terrain: a downhill makes it easy to break away.

- Weather: heading into the wind would be a deterrent.

- Your knowledge of the other athletes present: you need to know whether you'll have any competition when you break away

As a solo skater, you should expect to win when you break away on your own. Otherwise, you'll just end up with a worse time than you would have had by staying put.

Finishing Sprint

When you're skating an outdoor race, you sprint at the start and the end. Both arms are swinging. You remain in a deep crouch during your final sprint. Here is how your arms and legs should be moving:

1. Swing your arms more to the front, and always cross the body. Your arms should never come straight in front of you and straight back. Be sure your arms come at an angle across your body, so your right hand is over your left ear, and vice versa.

2. Your arm movements help you push to the side for more power. Use your legs to the utmost—sideways. Don't push with your toes—push with the sides of your skates, driving with your heel.

WHY HAVE TEAMS?

More and more racing teams are being formed. Skate manufacturers Rollerblade and K2 field teams, for example. These teams have a commercial purpose—to prompt audiences to try the sponsors' equipment. Teams also have a function in winning or strategy.

When teams race, it usually increases the chances that one of their members will win a race. In general, it's better to skate with a team than to skate solo. Often, if money is won, it's shared. Share the glory, the dollars, and the fun!

A possible drawback of team racing is that one individual is chosen to win by the team or its coach. You may like this approach, or you may not care to be told, "Today you're going to win." Worse, but possible: "Today, you're not going to win!" That's part of team racing, though.

ALLIES

You may choose to work with a friend in a race. Perhaps the two of you agree beforehand, "If we're both up near the front at the finish, we'll help each other—we'll let each other into the line." But it doesn't always work out that you and your friend are at the same ability and energy levels during the same race. One of you may be far ahead of the other. So don't count on your allies!

STRATEGIC TIPS

Arrive early and check out the course. Pick out the place where you will begin your sprint. In 10K and 20K races two skaters will lead the others. Perhaps a team of four or five out of a pack of twenty will form a strategy.

Two will stay behind and do their best to swerve in front of other skaters—blocking the pack. Meanwhile the two lead skaters will eventually be caught by the pack. When the lead skaters are caught by the pack, the two racers who had been behind will become the two "rabbits." They'll sprint ahead. Their friends will block for them.

This strategy tires out the pack.

Meanwhile one teammate is selected to win the event. That skater gets all the rest he or she needs before the final sprint.

In rare cases, one individual will skate without the pack and win. It's called breaking away. He or she doesn't benefit from drafting but can win. In most cases, the pack will catch these solo rabbits. People playing a pack strategy have to decide whether to catch the leader or stay behind and hope the original strategy works out.

Finding the Hole

To move up, you may have to find a hole in the pack. In the early stages of a race, others may let you into a hole. But as the competition grows more fierce and the finish approaches, you're more likely to be pushed out of the hole—or do some pushing yourself.

500-METER RACE

This is an all-out sprint. Grabbing and pulling can and does happen. Just listen to skate racer Derek Parra

describe the action at a 1993 500-meter race in Belgium (as quoted in *In-Line Magazine*): "I got grabbed by an Italian, who held onto me for about 10 feet. . . . At the Marathon '92 in Rome, the Dutch guys punched me in the back."

Parra, considered by many to be "the world's fastest man," is basically a nice guy. But he will fight to retain his position as the end of a race approaches. Grabbing, jostling, and jockeying seem to be a part of the sport and something that participants should expect—especially at the higher levels.

50K AND 100K—MARATHONS AND ULTRAMARATHON LONG DISTANCE

The original marathon was a foot race in Greece. Among runners, it's a 26-mile course. For in-line skaters, ultramarathons are races of 50K and longer.

Once you have mastered the outdoor 10K with a good, competitive time, you may want to consider entering the 50K and finally a 100K. While a 10K is like a fast sprint, longer races require a longer training buildup. Expect to spend several months in preparation for this grueling competition. Cross training will keep you from getting burned out.

The Athens to Atlanta Road Skating Marathon

Would you like to enter the most popular marathon of its kind? Then consider the Athens to Atlanta Road Skating

Georgia Marathon. That's an 85-mile trek, and it's held every October. This is a true ultramarathon. It's also the world's most recognized in-line skating event.

This mega-event began on quad skates 13 years ago, in October 1982. The race is organized by the Atlanta Peachtree RoadRollers, a local club that began in 1980. IISA does not sponsor this type of event, concentrating its energies on more popular races such as the 10K.

In the early years of this ultramarathon, there were no checkpoints or cars roaming to help out beleaguered racers. Checkpoints became standard in 1985.

Controversy is no stranger to this race. Dennis Bell won in 1986, but he used a moped as a personal support vehicle (someone riding nearby to provide water, etc.). It was alleged that he drafted the moped, and his time remains contested.

The Dutch, famous for being tough racers, made their presence known in 1991. Although their native country is flat, they had no trouble with American hills and finished as winners in both men's and women's categories.

In 1993, more than 250 people entered, compared to 150 in 1992. In 1994, 307 racers entered the competition. People come in from all over the United States and from countries such as Columbia, West Germany, Canada, Mexico, and Holland. The course record is held by a Dutchman, Haico Buma, who did the entire distance in under 4.5 hours, or 20 m.p.h.!

The event is held rain or shine. In 1992, rain poured steadily—but not hard enough to dampen racers' spirits. Times were slower, but that's the way it is with ultrama-rathons. Even an earthquake wouldn't impede these stalwarts—they'd just jump over a crevice!

The path includes all kinds of surfaces, smooth to rough. "It's a true road marathon," says Henry Zuver of IISA. "Traffic goes by, and skaters just stay single-file to one side of the road." His wife, Valerie Zuver, was one of the first women winners, taking first place in 1985.

All kinds of skates are allowed, including four- and five-wheeled in-lines and quad skates.

Corporations, including Hyper, Bauer, and Riedell, have supported the race since 1986.

The event attracts people from ages 8 to 70! Racers train for at least three-quarters of the distance they're doing several times before they skate the full distance. They skate comfortably at 60 miles before attempting this 85-mile trek.

Awards are given in seven age categories, for both sexes. Categories are 12 and under, 13–17, 18–29, 30–39, 40–49, 50–59, 60+. Skaters may also skate in full-distance and half-distance categories.

ORGANIZED COMPETITIONS

Two large organizations, USAC/RS and IISA, provide different forms of help and guidelines to skaters and racers.

USAC/RS

The United States Amateur Confederation of Roller Skaters has a speed-skating division. USAC/RS organizes indoor competitions and a limited number of outdoor sessions. USAC/RS races are on 100-meter tracks, and 1,000-meter races are common. People register in September with a particular club.

Regional or league competitions take place once a month. This is a way for skaters to gauge how they're performing and progressing. In June and July, each of nine regions has its regional meet. The top three regional finishers in each division go on to national competition; it adds up to a couple hundred athletes.

Racers who wish to further excel can go on to the Olympic Training Center. Competition there helps skaters qualify for World and Pan Am Games. The easiest way to get involved is to contact USAC/RS to find the nearest club.

IISA

IISA sanctions racing events, certifies speed-skating instructors, offers insurance, and publishes guidelines for various events, including races. This group will sanction rather than sponsor outdoor races.

Competition membership in IISA is available in several

WINNERS OF THE ATHENS TO ATLANTA 85-MILE SKATE

Year	Men	Time	Women	Time
1982	Keith Donaldson	*	no finisher	—
1983	Keith Donaldson	6:37:00	Ann Norelli	7:48:25
1984	Ken Taber	6:31:10	Ann Norelli	7:30:31
1985	Don Ruiz	6:44:00	Valerie Zuver	6:56:00
1986	Dennis Bell	6:11:33	Janice Phillips	12:03:32
1987	Uwe Brockmann	5:39:00	Ann Norelli	10:14:00
1988	Uwe Brockmann	5:15:00	Karen Edwards	5:45:00
1989	David Cooper	4:46:15	Diane Hayford	6:55:25
1990	Eddy Matzger	4:35:57	Karen Edwards	5:46:06
1991	Haico Buma	4:28:14	Karin Verhoef	5:32:54
1992	Eddy Matzger	5:02:36	Tammy Kesting	6:16:40
1993	Doug Glass	4:36:49	Dominique Laroque	5:41:48

Source: Atlanta Peachtree RoadRollers

*Time not recorded.

categories. Each category has its special requirements:

- *Super Elite.* This group includes men with a 10K time that is below 17:00. Women's 10K times must be below 19:00. However, IISA's Competition Committee (IISA/CC) may approve exceptions. This allows participants to compete in expert or elite events.

- *Category 1.* Men's time must be less than 18:30.

Women can skate the 10K at 20:30 or less. IISA/CC may approve exceptions. This allows participants to compete in expert events.

- *Category 2.* Here, skaters have to have skated a minimum of three sanctioned IISA/CC races. Men's times achieved must be less than 23:00 (25:00 for women).

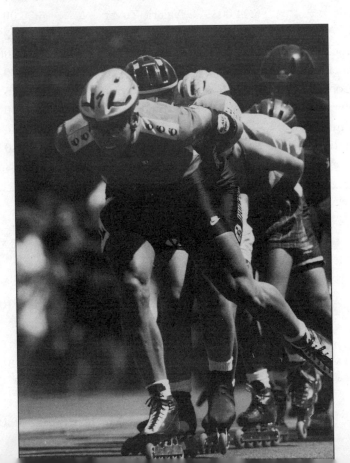

- *Category 3.* This entry-level competition membership allows skaters to compete in events designated for novices.
- *Sport.* This general kind of membership is usually given to officials and others who organize novice and noncompetitive events.
- *Junior.* This category includes skaters who are 14 or younger. They are permitted to compete only in novice and noncompetitive events.

IISA recreational members cannot compete in IISA sanctioned events without first moving up to Sport or Category 3 membership.

Age Groups

IISA recognizes fourteen age groups for their rankings at different levels and for the group's championships. Those divisions are

6 and under	35–39
7–10	40–44
11–14	45–49
15–17	50–54
18–24	55–59
25–29	60–69
30–34	70 +

Contact IISA to find a listing of clubs and to receive membership information (see Appendix A for address and telephone number).

INTERVIEW WITH DEREK PARRA, THE WORLD'S FASTEST SKATER!

Derek Parra, who was born in 1970, skates for Geo Rollerblade, along with five other men and four women. He races both indoors and outdoors, preferring outdoors. And no wonder—there, he is the two-time world champion, still reigning at the time of this interview.

Derek won the World Speedskating Championships in 1993 in Colorado Springs, Colorado, and again in 1994 in Gujan Mestras, France. In 1993, he beat out skaters from thirty countries fielding an average of four players per team. In France, in 1994, twenty-two countries were represented. Most teams had eight skaters, and so he came out ahead of more than 170 of the world's fastest in-line racers.

Tell us about the exciting championship race.

There were three days of racing on track and three days on road. Ten thousand plus people lined the asphalt track. It was exciting!

I won on the basis of accumulated points. In a run of 43 skaters, for example, you get 43 points if you win first place. At these races, they usually have a 200-meter banked track or a 400-meter oval, which is asymmetrical.

The event is organized in the U.S. by the USAC/RS and internationally by the Federation Internationale Roller Skating (FIRS), the governing body for all countries in roller skating.

How did you first get involved in skating?

I used to live in California, and I used to go to skating sessions. They offered free Cokes for racers. That was all it took! That was back in 1984, when I was 14. Then I joined a speed team that year. All of this was on conventional skates. I didn't get started on in-lines until about two years ago.

In the old days, no one ever used in-line for indoors, because the wheels were unsuitable. At 26 m.p.h. inside, we were leaning over like ice-skaters, and the wheels that were made three years ago wouldn't let you grip. In the last few years, wheel makers have allowed us to skate at more of an incline.

Before, on conventional skates, you had to skate above your skates, or you'd slip. Now with in-line, you can lean more to your left, to the inside of the track.

What kind of wheels do you prefer for indoors?

I like Hyper 80 mm, and the right surface. For indoors, on a 100-meter flat track, on a tight surface, I like a 97- to 99-durometer wheel. The rink managers roll on some urethane, too, which makes the floor grippy. It's like having fresh ice or sharpened blades on ice.

Outdoors, roads are rough. I need a softer wheel, a 78-durometer wheel with more rebound. You need more shock absorbency. I stick to an 80 mm.

I used to always use 76 mm, but now you can grip more on an 80 mm for indoors. The profile of the wheel is higher. We've been using 80s outdoors. I just did the New York City Skate Marathon, and myself and Boutiette got first and second place. In areas where there are big hills, though, I prefer a smaller 76-mm wheel—so it depends on the course.

What's the most common mistake you see outdoor racers making?

Some skaters break form at the end of the race. At the final sprint, they run on their skates. You don't have to move your feet 100 m.p.h.—instead of accelerating, you'll spin out. You don't gain any more speed by that. Sprint, with a full push in every stroke. It's like cyclists who never change gears. Some skaters are like that—a lot of people never change gears. They run on their skates, with arms moving back and forth, instead of side to side.

What's the most common mistake you see indoor racers making?

The biggest thing I see is not controlling their race. Some skaters will be nowhere near the lead with 200 meters to go or four corners to pass. There's not much time left to pass. They're in the back of the pack, rather than the front. That person uses twice as much energy passing two people than those near the lead. By the time the far-back skater moves up past one or two skaters, it's too late. People stay at the back too much. They wait too long to pass.

What other teams do you skate against these days?

There are about fifteen teams, with two or three major corporate-sponsored teams. K2 Skates sponsors skate shops, which then field teams. The national teams are Geo Rollerblade, Hyper, and K2 Skates. Labeda used to have a big in-line team, but now they're into hockey. Their wheels work great on a plastic tile floor, such as the RHI uses.

What kinds of cross training do you prefer?

I ride, run, do slide board, and skate indoors and outdoors. Some people on the U.S. Roller Speedskating

Team only skate. They don't do power training, weights, or anything. They've mainly skated all their life. A skater named Chad Hedrick, for example, skated all of his life. He just skates.

I cross train in part because I came into the sport late. Dante and Tony Muse were already national champions before I started skating, so I do catch-up. They have each other to race against—I don't. That's why I do all the hard bike rides. A bike also lets you sit, which lets you work your legs longer.

By not cross training, other racers are just using a different approach. It's not worse if it works for them. For instance, Dante Muse once tried training using my style, and it hurt him! His muscles couldn't handle it. He is the best when he trains his way. The most important thing is to learn your own body.

I can't get a hard enough workout indoors as I can outdoors biking.

To what do you attribute your success, and in what order of importance?

I'd say first of all my belief in God. I ask for God's blessing before the race and I thank him after the race. I pray each day for the blessings He's given me.

My will to win and compete is strong. I love skating and racing. My work ethic is important—training hard. And my coaches, who support me, plus my friends and family, who give me 100 percent.

Cross training and weight training are important, too. Cross training your muscles helps reduce monotony. I run to stay thin and to help my cardiovascular system. Running 4 miles hard is the toughest thing I do. I do a 4-mile loop in 27 minutes, and at the end of the year I do it in 21 minutes. Running helps me keep thin.

I do weights on my upper body—curls and dips and bench press. I do high reps, so that I don't build muscle mass. Weight holds you down.

INTERVIEW WITH WENDY KELLY

Wendy Kelly is an accomplished indoor racer. Spirited and unpretentious, she has achieved a great deal in a short amount of time. She shows by her example how

people with everyday jobs can excel—and have a ball while doing it!

Born in 1965, Wendy lives in Collingswood, New Jersey. Her preferred racing events are the 1,500-meter indoor and the 10K outdoor. Wendy is a member of the Omni Speed Club, a cofounder of Landskaters In-Line Skate Club, and a member of USAC/RS. In 1994 she was ranked fifth nationally for indoor racing by USAC/RS and ranked sixth by IISA for outdoor racing. Wendy is an accountant.

How did you first get interested in skating?

My husband, Doug, and I started to recreationally skate as cross training for skiing. Because I'm competitive in nature, I entered some races on four-wheeled in-line skates. I had raced a couple of races in the recreational division of area races.

A couple of people suggested I get five-wheeled skates. I said, "No, no, no, I don't want to get into it that deep." But by the end of summer of 1992, I was doing so well, I had won a pair of racing skates. So I said, "I guess I should do this!" In spring of 1993, when I got my equipment ready, I started competing at the elite level.

Did you then join up with a group or a trainer?

No, I still was on my own through April, May, June, and July. Then I met another girl who was competing and who was familiar with the indoor Omni rink in Voorhees, New Jersey; and she brought me to indoor skating. That's when I decided to try that—in September 1993. From then to August of 1994, I competed at the Omni. That's what got me to go to Nebraska and be ranked fifth.

How did you feel about the new, intense training?

It's a very large commitment; a majority of my club members are younger—13 through 17. I find that, as an adult, someone who's married, racing is very time-consuming. You almost have to give up your social life. You can't do much more than work and train.

How much time do you devote to training?

We practice four days a week, after work. Depending on the person, you should probably do a lot of cross training, too. I try to work out 6 days a week, sometimes twice a day. I have a husband, home, and job. I do a combination of skating and dry land exercises.

We do plyometric exercises. They're a type of motion you're putting your muscles through. It's almost a muscle-building type exercise. Squats are almost plyometric. We'll do lowering and raising exercises, to develop the quadriceps. It's also very good to ride a bicycle and jog. We're talking about five or six different training activities that racers are doing!

How many hours a day do you spend training?

One and a half to three per day. We sometimes go from indoor to outdoor practice.

What kinds of wheels do you prefer for indoor and outdoor?

For indoor, I prefer Sidewinders. They're 80 mm, and about an 85 durometer—pretty hard. For outdoor, I prefer Hyper Shocks, 80 mm, 78 or 82 durometer. Lots of frames don't fit an 82 mm wheel.

I'm sure there are different kinds of pleasures you get from racing. Tell us about them.

I love winning—that would always be one! I get a rush from competing. I have found myself in situations where I didn't realize I could go that fast.

Do you get a real kick out of passing people?

Yeah! It's a challenge to get back in the draft line. I like to sprint at the end. A lot of times, depending on the athletes that show up, you can hang out with the pack. A lot happens, and it's usually very exciting at the end. The rest of the race can be interesting or boring. Sometimes someone will pull ahead and stay there.

Do you find that women are more reluctant to compete, because they're taught to cooperate and not try to win?

Not the women I race with. One of my teammates had goals she wasn't meeting. When she finally won, she screamed out: "I knew I could do it!" The women I'm with are vocal, and they're not afraid to vocalize.

Do men racers treat women well?

I find I'm more welcome to compete. Guys want us there. So there's not much discrimination or intimidation. I have felt very welcome in the past two years I've been in

racing. Not only are you welcome to be out there, but guys are getting tired of looking at other guys! When we're not there, they often complain, "Hey, where are the women?"

The fact that Bonnie Blair made such an impression encouraged lots of women to realize that this is something you can do. At the same time, there's a ways to go yet—at a larger race, the men's field is usually three times larger than the women's. At a local race, men usually outnumber women by twice. But most of the outdoor teams have women now.

Is it wise to have separate men's and women's categories?

Yeah, there's no way that women can compete with men. Women don't get as much prize money as the men do, and I agree with that. Women's speeds aren't up to men's.

Do you feel racing is growing?

It's growing, but slowly, as far as indoors. The indoor field used to be a lot larger with traditional roller skates. Before three years ago, USAC/RS said you could only allow quad skates indoors. Quad racing indoors had been around for over 40 years. When they allowed in-line, a lot of good quad skaters dropped out. It was a totally different technique. Now quad and in-line are separated, as well as there being age distinctions.

What are some successful techniques for winning?

If you don't have technique, you can be the strongest person out there and you'll never win. Work on your technique! This includes everything. Your upper body has to fall over. It's very complicated like, say, volleyball.

There's just so much to know. It's very difficult to get everything in the line it's supposed to be in. The part of the foot you're pushing with is so important. When you cross your right over your left, then your left actually pushes to the right. That has to be done from the heel, or you won't get the full force.

Also, most people don't fall over enough—they wind up pushing from the toe. Your foot should be so flexed that it's practically off the ground. It's a hard position to put your body in. You have to get down almost in a sitting position as you're going around in a circle. Some newer skaters have a difficult time just balancing on one foot.

How would you rank technique, conditioning, strength, and strategy?

At this point, strategy is last. If you don't have the other areas, you won't be able to exercise them! I'd rank them exactly that way—technique, conditioning, strength, and strategy.

Do outdoor techniques have much overlap with indoor?

Yes, you use a lot of the same muscles, especially if you're on a course with a lot of crossing over. The skater who skates indoors has much more strength in doing that. The indoor skater accelerates on the turn, even when outdoors. Some outdoor skaters slow down on the turn. I used to have to drop back and try to catch up. It tires you out!

Eddy Matzger is one of the few top-ranked outdoor skaters who's not an indoor skater. That's because indoor gives you great training, and it's all year long. A lot of skaters, as soon as they get off the plane from nationals go right back to the rink and start practicing. People are really dedicated!

There's no monetary reward in indoor, and much less exposure. IISA helps outdoor skaters get publicity, which helps the sport grow. Indoor skating is not sponsored, except for World Team, which is sponsored by Rollerblade. So indoor racing is a total expense to the skaters. All of your equipment is a good 700 to 800 dollars, and you pay your coaches and the rinks. We went to an invitational, and we all paid our expenses there, too. Even at the nationals, we had to pay for all of it.

Do you enjoy even the training?

Oh yeah! I probably enjoy it more. I train as a lifestyle. I'm seriously into the way I feel. Training and racing are a part of my life, and I hope they always will be.

When you're out there huffing and puffing, are you thinking, "This is great!"?

Usually! I like to sweat! I work out with a personal trainer twice a week for 30 minutes with weights, on a super slow workout. It's a way of building muscle. It's high weight with repetition, at a slow pace.

I work seven movements for my whole body, including squats with a machine, evenly distributed on both shoulders. Then I do leg extensions—I'm sitting and weights are down on my ankles, and I lift my legs. In leg curls, I lie on my stomach, and the weights are down around my ankle. As I curl my leg back, I'm using the weight.

What would you say to people who are considering getting into racing?

Now that I've skated indoors and I see what it's like, I'd recommend becoming an indoor skater—even if you don't want to compete. Most coaches are open to people attending practices. In another year or so, skaters who are only outdoors won't be able to hang with those indoors. They also need to get involved in a training program with a lot of cross training. Weight training is important, too.

It's a good time to get in, because it's not really competitive yet! Women's racing is less competitive than you'd think. I've been skating just one summer, and I'm going to an Olympic Skating Center! In the year 2000 in Australia, in-line indoor racing will be an Olympic event.

What does racing do for your stamina and everyday energy level?

If you don't go overboard, it definitely raises it. If you do go overboard, you're exhausted all the time. Just the fact that you're involved in this sport—that you have an organized practice to go to and camaraderie with your teammates—that gives you energy, because you're excited to be involved!

Any sport is work. I feel good definitely during, and definitely after training and competing!

Laird McClure

12

SKATE DANCING AND FIGURE SKATING

*I*n-line dancing is a wonderful way to express, and enjoy, yourself on skates. It's both a sport and an art-form. You get a chance to teach your body new tricks, move to music, and grow in agility—all at once!

And that's just the skinny on the topic. Because there's so much to explore in in-line dancing, a chapter can only inspire you to go out and discover what it's all about for yourself.

Laird McClure

The waltz lives on in-line.

You may find that you're a pioneer locally in in-line dance. Take that as an opportunity and a challenge. You see, in-line dancing is a newcomer and not yet an established presence in the world of organized roller skating. So don't expect to find squadrons of artistic in-line dancers taking to the rink nearest you. This may change over time. Nevertheless, artistic in-line skating has grown in respectability on the national and international scene.

This chapter will tell you a bit about the development of the art to date, explain terminology, and show you how to perform artistic dance moves and develop your own routine.

THE ORIGINS OF SKATE DANCING

In-line dance skating derives in part from ice skating and, to some extent, from a quad roller-skating tradition. In-line artistic dancing uses the same terminology as figure skating on ice and artistic quad roller skating. As an artistic skater, you can draw upon the traditions and experiences of these sports.

A dancer named Scott Cramer, U.S. and World Professional Ice Skating Champion, produced a pioneer videotape that shows sixteen dances for in-line skaters. He and his partner have modified some of the U.S. Figure Skating Association dances, adapting them for in-line dancing. This tape, now available commercially, accomplished an important achievement—it helped inspire in-line skaters around the nation. (See Appendix B.)

There are few experts and sanctioning bodies to judge artistic in-line skating. Most people are involved in it for fun and as a form of artistic expression. The standards that do exist for in-line artistic skating are set by USAC/RS, which now permits in-liners to enter competitions. However, most prominent skate dancers use traditional quad skates.

The IISA is now developing a Class III certification for instructors. One of these certifications will be for in-line freestyle, dance, or artistic skating.

TYPES OF ICE-SKATE DANCING

As in-line skate dancing becomes more organized, participants tend to look to ice-skating tradition to establish norms. The main categories of traditional ice-skating divisions are:

- *Dance.* This form of dancing was made famous in the Olympics by ice-skaters Torvill and Dean. Moves include the use of edges to trace a set pattern on the ice. No jumps or spins are allowed, just skating on edges as a couple. The couple never jumps to leave the ground, and there are few lifts, no death spiral, and no throws, jumps, or spins.

- *Freestyle short program.* In this form of skate dance, the skater must complete a 2-minute technical program, in which required elements are performed.

- *Figures.* Here the skaters skate circular eights and a variety of turns and edging techniques, all performed on a clean sheet of ice. Skaters are then judged on their preciseness.

- *Freestyle singles.* This category features spinning and jumping and footwork, set to music, done by one person.

- *Freestyle pairs.* In pairs skating, side-by-side jumps are allowed. Skaters can also do side-by-side spins, big lifts, or full overhead lifts. Couples are also allowed to do pair spins, holding on to each other.

In other moves, such as side-by-side camel spins, the two skaters can be 6 or 7 feet apart.

IN-LINE DANCING AND ICE DANCING

There's one critical difference between in-line skating and ice dancing: The toe pick doesn't exist on an in-line skate. The only move that's hard to do well is a one-footed spin—only a couple of revolutions are possible before the wheel friction slows you down. Otherwise, you can do all of the jumps and the dance moves.

Doing the double-daffy.

Some manufacturers are developing toe-stop chassis designs that will extend far beyond the front wheel. This may not be a perfect solution—skaters need to have a sense that their toe stop is not too far in front of their front wheel.

Accomplished ice-skaters may go to great lengths to create a toe stop or something similar on their in-lines. They may insert a chunk of rubber where the front wheel normally rests. The piece of rubber allows certain toe jumps to be done, kicking off that toe for lift. The jump achieved with the aid of rubber (springy stuff!) can give more of a boost than that achieved by ice skaters using toe picks. Even double revolution toe jumps are possible on these home-made inventions!

IN-LINE DANCING AND ROLLER-SKATE DANCING

In general, in-line skate dancing remains more difficult than roller-skate dancing. This is especially so if you don't have the right skates—light, agile, ventilated ones.

People who begin dancing on quad roller skates stick with them. On the other hand, many who in-line dance tend to be ice-skaters looking for a similar feel.

ROCKERING HELPS!

If you take up artistic skating, you'll find that you gain agility by rockering your skates. You'll be reducing your turning radius, because only two or three wheels will be on the ground. With your second and third wheels lower, and the first and fourth wheels higher, you'll be able to cut a tighter circle.

No manufacturer has actually marketed a frame for in-line dancing—a three-wheeled frame with an adjustable toe stop in place of the front wheel. Any toe stop that is developed should be able to swivel, perhaps on bearings. This would assist toe spins.

TERMINOLOGY

There is much controversy concerning the terminology of dance and in-line skating. Some would say that *freestyle skating* is the proper term for dancing or other forms of artistic expression to music as done on in-line skates. Others argue just as heatedly for *in-line dance*, *artistic skating*, and yet other terms. Many of these terms overlap in meaning.

Because our goal in this chapter is to help you skate artistically in the way you find most enjoyable, I won't spend too much time on semantics. But allow me to explain the competing terms as skaters use them, and how they relate to each other:

- *Artistic dance skating.* This is any kind of dancing-type movement on skates, set to music. It can be improvised or choreographed and may include elements of freestyle skating. Artistic hand motions are used, emulating ice-skating on in-lines.

- *Freestyle skating.* Some people call skate dancing and freestyle the same thing. Freestyle includes gymnastic-type moves, spins, and even curb grinds. Hip-hop or rock music may be a part of a freestyle exhibition.

- *Skate aerobics.* High-intensity skate dancing, done for a good workout as well as for pleasure. Artistry is not as important here as is the cardiovascular workout achieved. Skate aerobics may also be viewed as skate dancing, done in a group.

- *Figure skating.* In this form of skating, various patterns are traced on the ground by the skate wheels. The sport began as a form of ice skating. Traditional roller skaters have also developed the sport for many decades.

Figure skating used to be limited to "school figures." This meant tracing a circle in the ice surface using the inside and outside edges. Figure skating uses the body to create the figures, or circles—the skates become a kind of writing instrument.

Pure figure skating has experienced a decline in popularity, relative to other forms of artistic skating. People who can do double and triple axels sometimes have trouble with tracing the circle! Since the 1992 Winter Olympics, school figures have been dispensed with.

- *Pairs skating.* This form of figure or artistic skating involves more lifts and fancy steps. Skating apart from each other is permitted, but skaters usually mirror or shadow each other's movements. Standards for judging pairs dancing include types of moves performed, how well they are done, creativity in expressing the music, skill in connecting the moves to form a unified whole, and ability to impress a crowd.

- *Dance skating.* In ice skating, this sport has many requirements. Contact must be maintained through most of the routine. The partner may not be lifted above the shoulders. Separate routines are not allowed. Jean Torvill and Christopher Dean popularized dance skating by achieving extraordinary scores at the 1984 Winter Olympic Games at Sarajevo, Yugoslavia.

WHY LEARN IN-LINE SKATE DANCING?

The best reason to start skate dancing is because *you believe you'll enjoy it*—the fluid grace of wheel and surface, bodies in sinuous movement together, and the merging of music and form. If that excites you, go for it!

USAC/RS has started setting standards for in-line dancing—a natural outgrowth from its decades of involvement in quad dancing. IISA has not been greatly involved, although it may soon be. However, manufacturers and stores often provide support and promote demonstrations. For example, Camp Rollerblade includes skate dancing.

The Pure Fun of Skate Dancing

Skate dancing need not be done in an organized setting, with rules and judges. You can skate as a form of self-expression, just doing what your legs want and your heart demands.

We can call this fun dancing, although it's also known as street dancing or freestyle dancing. The challenge here is to find music you like—it must have that certain *je ne sais quoi* (unknown ingredient) so that you will truly live the music and make your routine come alive.

Laird McClure

Another consideration in choosing music is the *length* of the piece and its *development*. A tune that lingers too long may tax your ability or interest. A piece that's too brief might stop just when you're getting in the groove. You may want a piece with multiple rhythms—giving you a chance to show off different styles and moods. For these and other reasons, it's critical to match your artistic ambition perfectly with your music.

To develop your dancing moves, first choose your music. Then, depending on what feels right to you, either improvise to the music and write down what you've done or write a list of moves and then try to execute them to the music. You might also try starting with a list of moves and then perform them to the music. See where the moves feel right and where the music seems to "call" for them. Developing formal routines is discussed later in this chapter.

Getting Started

The best way to learn artistic dance is to train with an expert. To find the right person, contact the major national skating organizations or go to your local stores. They're in contact with local trainers. If one store can't help you, try another. A hint: owners are usually not as helpful as people who are into skating.

You'll find another resource to be your local skating rink—and the quad skaters who dance there. You can imitate them on your in-lines. Strike up a conversation with these folk. They'll probably clue you in to local skate-dancing contacts.

SPECIAL EQUIPMENT

Because of the demands made by artistic skating, the equipment can vary from that used by recreational in-line skaters.

Boots

Rollerblade Aeroblades are very popular among freestyle artists and skate dancers. They are very light, and you can get a secure fit with buckles. They're also ventilated and flexible. Aeroblades have four wheels and are easily rockered. Sizes 6 and below employ only three wheels.

As with other dance-oriented skates, the use of larger center wheels in the rockered position will help you in dance and freestyle moves.

Try to avoid the mistake many people make of choosing their dance skates blindly. If you rush, you may spend $200 on the wrong skates, whereas the right pair for skate dancing may actually be less expensive. Take your time, and try on several brands, sizes, and models.

The most significant qualities in a skate are comfort, snugness, and agility. Having a lot of play in your skates does not provide comfort. Aeroblades and Coolblades are fine for dancing. Coolblades have a thinner liner, which you may prefer. Although big, heavy skates are fine for normal recreational skating, they could feel clumsy when dancing.

Team Geo Rollerblade uses TRS Lightning skates, though they are heavier, lace-up, and with only one buckle on top. Smaller Lightning sizes have three wheels, which are hard to use when rockered.

The key qualities to look for in a dance skate are:

- *A very snug fit.* Skate liners made of Memory Foam (such as those used for Aeroblades) will mold to the contour of the foot. Consider going to a physician or a local ski or skate shop for orthotics, inserts customized for your foot. Hockey players and skiers know how to fit a boot—they tend to look for a smaller, tighter fit that won't stretch out excessively with use. Be sure to wear thin socks when trying on skates for in-line dancing.

- *Toes close to touching the end.* You need a snug fit that will not tax your feet. Don't judge the fit of a skate the way you judge a shoe; your toes should be close to the toe end of the boot.

- *Light weight.* Clunky skates make it hard to move gracefully!

- *Ventilation.* Look for plenty of air holes. Especially if you skate-dance indoors, you'll be building up heat.

- *Flexibility.* Your skates should not feel like ski boots. You need less ankle support and more flexibility.

Toe Stops

Some skates can accept toe stops that extend beyond the toe of the boot (see the comparison of in-line dancing to ice dancing on page 153). In principle, these adapted skates can make it easy to push off and do jumps. But many experienced dancers find the retrofitted toe stop to be poorly designed and ultimately an impediment.

Wheels

Wheels of 52 mm are good for dance and artistic skating: These are smaller than the 70- to 80-mm wheels used for recreation, hockey, and racing. The best durometer for in-line dancing comes down to a matter of personal preference. Many skate-dancers prefer a hard durometer, such as 96 compared to the normal 78. The harder the wheel, the easier it is to slide. Others, however, such as Jill Schulz and Team Rollerblade, prefer softer wheels. Try different wheels out with various moves and surfaces and decide for yourself which durometer suits your needs.

Beware: The hardness that makes it easier for you to slide will also make it easier to fall. So be careful your first time out on the new, harder wheels. You do need to be able to slide to execute many moves, including spins.

SKATE-DANCING MOVES

The moves described in this chapter will help you begin skate dancing. To fully explain all of the intricacies and many other moves, routines, and dances would fill an entire book. In fact, such books have been written—for ice-skaters.

If you are intrigued by what you read here, follow up by finding books on ice dancing and figure skating.

Skating backward, crossover turns, the daffy (toe-heel skating), and hourglass (or sculling) are covered in Chapter 7.

One-Footed Curve Glide

This move involves turning while gliding on one foot. Mastering the four varieties of this turn will help you develop a sense of your edges and how to ride them. The four basic glide turns are (1) skating on your right foot, curving to your right, (2) skating on your right foot, curving to your left, (3) skating on your left foot, curving to your right, and (4) skating on your left foot, curving to your left.

To glide one-footed:

Charlie Pruett

1. Extend your arms, keeping fingers together and extended in a graceful manner.

2. Bend your
knees.

4. Lift your trailing
leg in the air
behind you.

3. Lean forward and
place most of your
weight on your
balancing leg.

5. Lean into a turn by
riding a chosen edge.
Leaning right will
take you rightward,
and left leftward.

One-Footed Backward Glide

While you are skating backward, as demonstrated in Chapter 7, enter the one-footed backward glide by doing the following:

1. Extend your arms out and to the side for balance.
2. Increase pressure on your right foot. Bend your right knee.
3. Extend your left foot back behind you and off the ground. Straighten your left leg. You're gliding!
4. Repeat/alternate by placing weight on your left foot and lifting your right foot.

Shoot the Duck

1. Skate forward, while keeping your feet parallel to each other.
2. Bend down deeply, almost sitting on your heels. Keep your arms extended in front of you. Practice getting into this position and gliding.
3. Extend one leg in front of you.

If it's hard to keep your extended leg up, it's okay to support it with your hands.

The Bunny Hop

This move is simply a jump, with no turn or twist:

1. Skate forward and glide.

2. Place your weight on your left foot.
3. Swing your right foot back behind you, and off the ground, while bending your left knee. You're cocking this leg, getting ready for a kick.
4. Kick your right leg forward, thrusting your entire body into the air.
5. Land on both feet!

Two-Toe Glide or Toe Wheelie

You'll need excellent balancing skills to do this one, but it's a fun move. Here's how:

1. Skate forward on flat ground.
2. Place one leg behind the other.
3. Get up on the toes of your rear foot.

Toe wheelie.

4. Lean forward and extend your arms sideward for added balance.

5. Rise slowly on your forward toes. Arch your body backward and bend your knees. You've done it!

Spins

This move dizzies you as it dazzles onlookers. As with many freestyle-type moves, do it on flat ground for ease. The spin is done on the toe of one skate and the heel of the other. Your heel brake will get in the way of spins, so you should remove it. Be ready to stop some other way. (See Chapter 6 for stopping options.)

To spin, using a leftward or counterclockwise spin, as an example:

1. Choose a spot ahead of you as the site of your spin.

2. Move slowly toward the spot. For a leftward spin, before you arrive at your spot, cock both arms rightward.

3. Whip your arms and upper torso leftward, while placing your right foot slightly ahead of your left.

4. Lift your right toe up and your left heel up at the same time, and spin!

With practice, you can get several revolutions out of one spinning thrust.

Charlie Pruett

Spread-Eagle Turn

This turn is excellent for changing directions gracefully. You begin by skating forward and end up skating backward, as shown here by Nick Perna.

Charlie Pruett

1. Skate and glide on your right inside edge. Keep your arms extended and to the side.

2. Lift your left leg and angle your body sideward, toward the left.

3. Reposition your left skate so it's facing backward, with your left heel next to your right heel. Both skates should now be lined up. Your right skate points forward and your left backward. Hey, you're spread-eagled!

4. Lift your right foot, and swivel your body further to the left— so that you arrive in a skating-backward position.

5. Drop your right foot down, and skate backward.

Arabesque

This move is similar to a one-footed glide—but with several spoonfuls of grace and artistry added! All of your body soars in this move, except for one supporting leg.

1. Skate forward and glide on your left leg. Try to keep most of your body weight on the heel.

2. Raise your right leg behind you as you bend over, extending your arms to the side.

3. Arch your back. Act like you're happily "flying" through the air, with your face up. Keep your raised leg stiff as it moves behind you.

4. Glide straight or in a curved line.

Mohawk Turn

This turn is very similar to the spread eagle, except that in mid-turn both feet do not touch the ground at the same time. Here's how to do it, in a leftward turning manner:

1. Skate and glide on your right inside edge.

2. Raise your left leg and sweep it out to the side and behind you, rotating your left leg so that your foot points nearly backward. Your left skate should not yet touch the ground.

3. In a single turning, twisting motion, place your left foot down and lift your right foot. You're skating backward on your left foot now.

4. Drop your right foot and skate backward.

The arabesque as performed by Dwayne Vonfraenkel and Judi McClure.

Mapes

The mapes is a backward 360-degree jump spin. Done well, it is graceful and impressive, especially when combined with a backward arabesque.

1. Skate backward.

2. Lift your left leg in front of you, as you prepare to use it as a pendulum for turning and lifting. Bend your right knee slightly.

3. Swing your left leg back, sweeping past your right leg.

4. Just a few inches into your sweep, rocket your left leg downward—toe pointed toward the ground.

5. Jump into the air, rising off your left leg. Simultaneously twist your right leg leftward. Keep your face pointed backward until your body is completely into the turn.

6. Rotate 360 degrees, while drawing your arms together, forming them into an open circle.

7. Land on your right foot, with your right knee bent. Spread your arms out to the side as you land, for balance and grace.

8. If you like, enter a backward arabesque.

Charlie Pruett

360 Jump

The jump turn gives your routine a spectacular flourish. It's definitely worth adding to your repertoire. This description of a leftward spin can be reversed for rightward rotations:

Charlie Pruett

3. Whip your arms and torso leftward, while jumping.

4. Spin 360 degrees and land in a direction that continues and completes your turn.

CHOOSING MUSIC AND DEVELOPING YOUR ROUTINE

There are no firm rules for putting together in-line dance routines, since the art is still shaping itself. Start with music you enjoy dancing and moving to; music you enjoy will inspire you to move with grace and enthusiasm.

You can find guidance in the music traditionally used for ice-skating routines.

If you're following an ice-skating format, look for music with a change of tempo. Most skating programs start fast, have a slow section, and end with a fast section — though some skaters alternate in a slow/fast/slow pattern.

Many classical music compositions work well for both in-line and ice skating. Popular classical selections and composers include:

- Ravel's "Bolero"
- Mozart, especially selections featured in the movie *Amadeus*
- Selections by Stravinsky, Beethoven, and Vivaldi

1. Skate and turn left.
2. Cock your arms rightward while bending at the knees.

Show tunes that work well include selections from *A Chorus Line*, *Oklahoma*, *Cats*, *Starlight Express*, *Beauty and the Beast*, and *Annie*. Overtures from musicals work particularly well.

Rock, country, and jazz are usually not used, except in show programs such as Ice Capades or Parade of Champions. Victor Petrenko skated to "The Twist" in a show program, for example.

Most programs are composed of cuts and splices of various works. These cuts and splices for skating are an art form unto themselves. In competitive ice skating, for example, music studios are hired to work intensively on custom-edited selections.

Should you aspire to be a world-class in-line skater, you will also need to work with a trained choreographer to do a world-class program. Dance programs for Olympic-level ice skating take months to work out.

In-line dancing can be a great new source of pleasure for you—a way to relax with friends, feel in tune with your body, and even develop the entertainer living within you!

How you develop your skills and in *what direction* is entirely up to you in this wide open art and sport. The field stands open to trailblazers, and one of them might just be you.

INTERVIEW WITH NICK PERNA, IN-LINE DANCE SKATER EXTRAORDINAIRE!

Born in 1960, Nick Perna is one of the nation's leading in-line dance skaters. He has worked full-time as an ice-skating instructor since the age of 20, teaching mostly figure skating, but hockey too. He lives in Manassas, Virginia, with his wife and two young daughters, ages 4 and 2. They both in-line skate!

He has taught in-line skating, too, since 1990, at beginning skaters' schools and to competitive ice-skaters who want to use in-lining as a cross-training tool. He has performed for "Kids on a Roll," a Virginia-based program. He has also conducted several in-line seminars for IISA teachers, on in-line in general and on freestyle and figure skating.

Courtesy of Alice Berman, *Skater's Edge*

Skaters from around the country turn to Nick for training. Organizations of different kinds seek his help in setting guidelines for the development of in-line artistic dance.

Before we get into the serious questions, let me ask about your daughter — how can a 2-year-old possibly skate on in-lines?

I made in-line skates just for her! I took girls' hockey skates made for ice skating in a size 6, and I cut the blade off. Then I bought a pair of tiny, cheap in-line skates, cut them down, and attached them to the former ice skates. Now people ask about it when they see it!

How did you get involved with in-line dancing?

It grew out of my ice dancing. I tried in-line skates several years ago, when they were heavy and clunky. But they didn't feel enough like ice skates. When Rollerblade came out with the Lightning line, with a lighter boot and bearings, I got interested in using them.

Back then, people even said "You can't skate backward on them." That wasn't true! I then introduced the new skates to my ice-skating students. As far as I'm concerned, they're almost identical.

Does the fact that in-lines can be enjoyed off a rink give them a lot of appeal?

One of the biggest appeals is that you're not limited by a rink — *the whole world is a rink!* I ask my daughter, "Why don't you want to go to the ice rink?" She says, "Because we can just go outside!" Of course, there are a lot of people who like the indoor controlled atmosphere of a rink.

Interest in in-line dance seems to be growing fast — is that also how it looks to you?

Oh yeah, most definitely. The ice-skating industry has helped in-line and vice versa. More people are also learning to play hockey and figure skate — it's gotten big.

How are the major skating organizations viewing in-line dance and freestyle? And what are the governing bodies involved?

Right now, the governing body of ice skating is the USFSA, the U.S. Figure Skating Association. That's the national governing body for professionals and amateurs — mostly amateurs. In order to go to the Olympics, you have to start with USFSA tests to qualify for competitions.

Winners of first levels, the regional championship, go to the sectional championship. Winners of sectionals go to U.S. national championships. Those winners go to the world championships or Olympic games depending on whether it's an Olympic year or not.

In-line skate dancing has no governing national body. I wish there was. In fact, there's so much ignorance on what you can do on the figure end of in-lines that it's very frustrating. A lot of people don't even know you can do figure skating — including in-line skate manufacturers!

The IISA is working on a Level III Certification for instructors. Level III may be a step up from Level II. Level

IV may be sport-specific, such as dance and figure skating, ramp and vert, hockey, and speed skating. I'm working on guidelines this fall and winter, with the IISA.

USAC/RS decided not long ago that they wanted in-line skaters in their organizations. They'll allow in-line skaters to compete with quad skaters head-to-head. But because roller skaters can do certain spins and double and triple jumps, it's an unfair competition—and you won't see anybody doing it on in-lines. I think there needs to be a dance/artistic division with USAC/RS, where in-liners go against other in-liners.

The field is basically wide open and not organized. There are a lot of people looking for instruction and performance, and organizing events, and no one is doing it. There has yet to be an organized in-line figure-skating competition, amateur or pro, anywhere in the country!

Do in-line dancers have any advantages over quad skaters?

There are some moves—such as toe-edge work—that in-liners can do up on their toes, but quad skaters can't because they have a stopper up on their toes. In-line dancing on the floor looks more graceful than quad—in-liners can move quicker. It also has an edge quality that you don't get on quad. Plus, it's quieter! It's a lot more like ice skating.

In your opinion, who are the national leaders in in-line dance?

I would say myself, Jill Schulz, too. She's one of them, also from a figure-skating background. Many people take a streetstyle look. The figure-skating look has been completely untapped, because people think you can't do these jumps and skates.

Most streetstyle is geared toward launch ramps and curb grinds and stunts . . . stair riding. This is not done to music. Some people also do hip-hop. For example, Carolyn Bradley, up in New Hampshire. She's a former Team Rollerblade camp member and a former figure skater.

What's the best way to get started in in-line dance?

Find a good instructor! A student of mine, Dwayne Vonfraenkel, makes a 3-hour drive to learn in-line skate dancing, because there's no other way to do it. There's just no place. I had a young man who tracked me down from Augusta, Georgia. He's almost taking lessons over the phone. He's only 16, and he's so frustrated!

The best way is to get a pair of skates that fits you properly—do not get cheap equipment—or rent a good pair. I recommend TRS Lightnings, or Aeroblades, which is what I use. Bauer makes good equipment, but I haven't tried them. Then find a certified IISA instructor in a group format or a private format and take some lessons in basic skating.

If you can't find somebody who teaches advanced in-line figure-skating-type moves, such as done by an ice-skater—then take ice-figure-skating lessons. Don't go to a hockey coach! Most ice-skating instructors have been on in-line skates. If you learn to ice-skate, you can transfer it to in-line with a little bit of practice.

At your level of achievement, what are the main ways in

which in-line dance differs from ice dancing? And what are some of the best ways of compensating for in-line dancers' inability to slide sideways and jump off a toe stop?

Many people think that in-line skating has more limitations, but that's not true, except for a few ways. There are a lot of tricks that can be done with that wheel on the front and back of the skate. Even on hockey skates, you can't do it the way you can on an in-line skate.

The in-line skate offers you a chance to do some fancy tricks on your heels and toes. For example, you can do a spread eagle way up on your heels . . . which has a whole different look to it—very impressive!

If you have an instructor who's used to assembling programs, he has a better knowledge of what works well. Then you want to put your program together so that it appeals to a rink set-up. You want to cover a rink-sized area. A normal ice rink is 200 feet by 85 feet. Since there are no guidelines for us, it may be any size!

What moves do you consider essential to learn?

All skaters should know how to use all of their edges, forward, backward, left and right foot, inside and outside.

What are unusual or difficult moves?

The spins would include two-foot spins, cross-foot spins on heels and toes, and pivots. At this point, you cannot do sit spins and flying camels, the way you can on ice. I've worked with a lot of people on toe stops for in-line skates, but there's nothing to duplicate the spinning motion of ice. The skates do their job too well—they grip so well, too well to twist.

Jumps would include the waltz jump, salchow, loop jump, and the axel, named after Axel Paulsen—those are the edge jumps. Toe jumps include toeing in with your wheels to vault, and those that are doable include toe loops, flip jumps, and lutz jumps.

What kinds of people are entering in-line dance? Are there main interest groups?

Nobody does ice dance patterns such as fox-trot, rumba, tango, Kilian. This is compulsory dance—only Dwayne Vonfraenkel does it.

Most people want to learn figure-skating movements, such as crossovers and free turns. Most want to do it to music eventually. People will do this in streets and parking lots, and that's a shame, because there's no place to demonstrate. Street skaters can shred up a park—we can't! No one's even come out with a figure-skating-specific boot yet.

What can an in-line skater do about the absence of toe picks or stops?

On a quad skate it's called a toe stop, and on an ice skate it's a toe pick. All attempts to put a toe stop on an in-line skate, to simulate a toe pick, have, in my opinion, been misguided, because they're ahead of the front wheel. They should be instead of the front wheel. I've actually done it. I have a prototype, but I'm so busy with everything else, that I can't get it out there.

INTERVIEW WITH FREESTYLE SKATER JILL SCHULZ

Before she became an in-line skater, Jill Schulz was a U.S. Figure Skating Association Gold Medalist in ice figure skating and ice freestyle.

Now she skates for Geo Team Rollerblade, along with A. J. Jackson. She and A. J. Jackson were the first performers with Team Rollerblade in 1986–87.

She began her work with Team Rollerblade by traveling with a group of skaters in a demo van in California. A. J. and Jill did much to improve performance capabilities on skates. Together, they worked on choreographing and creating a team.

As a professional ice-skater, Jill has worked with Ice Follies, Holiday on Ice, Radio City Music Hall, and Universal Amphitheater.

Between figure skating and in-line skating, she worked as a professional actress and dancer. Jill has also appeared in many commercials on traditional roller skates.

How would you describe the kind of skating you do?

The skating that I'm particularly known for is very close to the sport of figure skating in both figure-skating and roller-skating tricks, but with a little more of a street edge and a more contemporary style than a figure skater would use.

What are some of the moves that you use that are different from an ice figure skater?

It's not so much moves, but the style in which we do them. One we do that is actually different is a 360 jump. Our spins are done on two feet, as opposed to one. We rotate on one toe and heel or both toes. Some people do them on both heels, which is uncommon—it's not that interesting of a spin. In context of performance, I do a lot of pair skating with Chris Mitchell.

Do you feel that there is not yet a perfect skate for spinning?

Courtesy of Rollerblade Inc.

No. It's not the boot that has anything to do with it. What's needed is more of a skate with a frame and a wheel that allows you to turn on the center. You'd only be spinning on one inch of the blade. On ice, you spin in a small circle in a tiny radius. You just can't get that kind of spinning motion with wheels on cement.

Can you do spins on in-lines?

In a good spin in ice skating, the toe pick doesn't even hit the ice. You don't even touch the ice, except for a scratch spin, done with one leg over the ankle and spinning very fast.

On in-line skates some people can get eight to ten revolutions out of a spin on the frontmost wheel, up on toe. But it's not anything that anyone spends much time on, and it's not an artistically inviting position. In ice skating, you don't spin on a toe, you spin on your edges.

Are you a freestyle or streetstyle skater?

I call street skating "streetstyle." I call anything with rail grinds and curb grinds "street." Anything with fun boxes and launch ramps is street. Freestyle is anything using tricks derived from competitive figure skating and roller skating.

Is freestyle more of an accepted event at both demos and competitions?

Freestyle has only been used in performances. There really haven't been many competitive events. It hasn't been developed in that direction at all yet. It's used almost exclusively by the Team Rollerblade freestyle skaters, formerly known as the Dance Team. We used to be heavier on dance, and now we're more into freestyle.

Did you used to do more dancing on skates?

It was more funk and hip-hop. But we added the team because of people willing to do the part-time work—they were more dancers than skaters. Now the majority of our skaters are ex-figure skaters and roller skaters with gymnastic abilities.

Is freestyle more recognized by the major skating organizations?

Not really. It's not recognized much at all, actually. Roller hockey and vert have become more popular. Racing is a little less popular.

Do you feel more should be done to develop freestyle or dance?

As a competitive sport, I'm not sure. I see it as an opportunity to work as professional in-line skaters in performance venues. All of the venues currently carry ice skating and puppet shows, and such. Why not add in-line skating shows with freestyle and aggressive skating, all choreographed as entertainment?

We've done some shows ourselves in Santa Rosa and at Knott's Berry Farm, and they were very well received. Crowds at Knott's Berry Farm Theater were 1,500 per show. In Santa Rosa, it was small as well, with 750 per show. We were testing it out on a small scale, and the response was excellent.

Do people come to you around the country to say, "How can I become a freestyle skater or dancer?"

People mainly ask how they can be on Team Rollerblade! That's the only way to in-line freestyle professionally right now. A few regional teams are doing it a bit. In vert and street, there are some regional teams that are not Team Rollerblade yet are very talented. They're professional in the sense that they're getting paid. A lot of talent is out there in vert. Not as much is out there in freestyle.

Is in-line figure skating popular?

You can't separate freestyle and figure skating completely. At Camp Rollerblade, which I produce and direct each year, we have classes in freestyle that are quite popular. But there's not much incentive to learn it. People a little older who always loved figure skating learn to do it on in-line skates.

What are some of the moves and tricks you feel a beginner should master?

The basics are forward and backward crossovers in both directions, 3-turns, and Mohawks. A good exercise is edging on one foot in a

straight line. It's a good strength and balance exercise.

What are some of the more advanced moves you use in your routines?

Some of those would be 360 jumps, spins, toe-toe and heel-toe, and pair moves. Some of the most basic ones would be forward inside death spirals. The man is on one foot and has you by the left wrist. The girl's body is laid completely out with the left ankle crossed over the right ankle, and the guy is spinning her around.

Axels we use, but not lutzes, because they use a toe pick. An axel is also called a 540, a one-and-a-half-turn jump. There's also a throw axel, where your partner throws you into the air and you do one and a half turns and land.

What are some of the real crowd-pleasers?

People love all of the overhead lifts! Anything where the girl is overhead. We do a star lift, a Detroiter, a platter, and a helicopter.

We also do a variety of moves where a guy throws a girl in a variety of lifts. Our biggest crowd-pleasing move is one our pair skating team does. We had four teams doing this trick at one time. It's called a bounce spin. The guy holds you by the ankles and spins you around. The girl is down by the side, and it looks like your head is going to hit the ground! I'd like to add that this is an extremely dangerous trick that should be used by professionals only.

Do audiences like to see risk-taking?

Yeah! Audiences like danger. We do a lot of tricks with a girl at the end of a whip in a death spiral, and a guy does a 180 over her head. Three are in the spiral, and each time she comes around he jumps over her.

The IISA is considering setting standards for dance and certification. Are you involved in that?

No, but I'm available.

What are the ideal skates for freestyle?

I would say a Lightning TRS or a Tarmac CE. The Rollerblade aggressive skate is the Tarmac. Then there's me, who skates in the old original Lightning, which laces up all the way. I liked it so much, I never changed. I like laces better.

What size and durometer wheels do you favor?

I prefer the Hyper Fat Boys, 72 durometer and 80 durometer. Not extra big or small, 72 mm. In freestyle, you want a little softer wheels. Team Rollerblade freestyle skaters prefer 80 durometer wheels, which grip well on small stages and through a lot of use of edges.

How do you see the future of in-line dance, artistic skating, figure skating, and freestyle?

It's hard to say right now, because there's really no one out there creating a competitive area of involvement for people. My particular interest is more opportunities for performance on skates. It's still a difficult area. As far as creating competition, it's so similar to figure skating and roller skating, but there are some limitations. There's no Olympics for it.

People go from learning dancing skills to performing and videos. That's a more reasonable direction for in-line skating to go. People need an incentive.

Do you have a certain number of routines?

We create new routines each year. There are sequences I always use in the choreography, but we're constantly developing new moves. There are a few set moves, and then we create new ones. I have a pair routine now with Chris Mitchell. It's two to two-and-a-half minutes long. Usually, all our music is hard-hitting and fast. This year, we skated to "Enigma," an alternative music number that's slower. It's romantic, kind of.

Do people relate to romance in skate dancing?

People relate in performance to hitting emotions, whether it's laughter or romance. It's one of the keys to successful entertainment. In a number such as the one Chris and I did, romance is important. Others are more action and excitement.

I take it you enjoy it all!

I enjoy doing both!

Are there newer tricks?

Some involve four people, rather than two. Even crack-the-whip involves four or five people. There's a four-person flipout. Everyone's going in a circle, four people holding hands. They're skating on their inside edges.

The girl's facing out. She leans back and lowers her head inside the circle and lifts one foot off the ground. She then drops into a death spiral; the other girl reaches her foot across and puts it on the wrist of the girl holding a guy's hand. She lets her head drop down and swings her foot up and over outside the circle. Now she's upside down, and the circle's moving the whole time. She flips out and ends up standing.

That move actually comes from artistic roller skating. There used to be competitions called Fours, with groups of four, and that's where that comes from. In roller skating, they call it artistic skating.

How important is gymnastics to what you do?

We use cartwheels, back flips, back handsprings. They're all crowd-pleasers. Totally!

13

RAMPS AND RAMP PLANS

*L*ike your skateboarding brethren, you may enjoy taking to the air. Riding a pipe is the shortest path to aerial freedom! Ramp tricks are described in Chapter 7.

In this chapter, you will learn how to build three kinds of ramps. Each serves a special purpose:

- *Jump ramps* get you in the air fast. You skate on a straightaway, ride up the ramp, then launch—and land on your feet!

- *Quarter-pipes* are curved surfaces that you can

ride up and down laterally—meaning you can skate across their surface. A quarter-pipe positioned against a wall can also help you get perpendicular so that you can wall-ride.

- *Half-pipes* are for true ramp masters and lovers of air. These are the monster U- or C-shaped ramps that provide plenty of curved and vertical surface. Skaters rock back and forth from one edge (called a *lip*) to another. A skater who flies off the edge of a ramp is said to be "getting air."

A cautionary note: Skaters working on ramps need to take extra measures to prevent injury. Wear all of the protective gear recommended in Chapter 3. Additionally, wear a special helmet made for ramp skaters, with extra forehead and back-of-neck protection. Also consider wearing hip pads, especially at the beginning. Never attempt moves that you haven't worked up to in stages.

Where at all possible, learn ramp and other skating moves from an experienced certified instructor. Use this book as a complement to, not substitute for, the personal training you receive.

EQUIPMENT NEEDED

The tools you'll need to build all of the ramps described in this chapter are common ones:

- Circular saw
- Scroll saw
- Hammer
- Screwdriver
- Power drill
- Eye goggles

All these items are readily found. Materials may be more expensive. But built right and properly maintained (coated and recoated with wood preservative and/or urethane), your ramp will last for years.

To keep your ramps lasting long outdoors, you should purchase exterior plywood, which will last longer than interior plywood. Pressure-treated exterior plywood would be best, but it's probably too expensive for you to use in the larger projects described in this chapter.

A sheet of ⅜-inch exterior pressure-treated plywood may cost you $46 a sheet, compared with $27 for plain exterior plywood. It might make sense for you to use the more expensive grade lumber for some small ramps that use little wood. To compensate for the lack of pressure treating, you can waterproof your plywood. Also be sure to apply urethane to riding surfaces.

You've got the tools and, as we say in Philadelphia, the right at-tee-tood. Now let's build!

BUILDING THE JUMP RAMP

Jump ramps will get you in the air, launching you up and forward, beyond the edge of the ramp. They are also called launch ramps.

Materials

- Plywood, ⅝ inch—4 sheets, 4 feet by 8 feet
- Plywood, ⅜ inch—1 sheet, 4 feet by 8 feet
- Plywood, ¼ inch—1 sheet, 4 feet by 8 feet
- Plywood plank, cut to 4 feet by 8 inches
- Two-by-fours—six 8-foot lengths
- Power and hand tools
- Nails or wood or deck screws

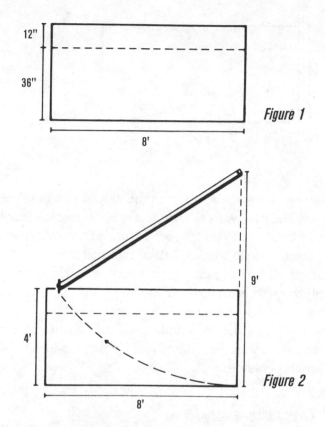

Figure 1

Figure 2

Step 1: Cutting Four Upright Supports

The hardest and most critical part of building your jump ramp will be marking the cut lines on your supporting plywood structures.

Start out with a sheet of 8-foot by 4-foot ⅝-inch plywood, positioned horizontally. Mark a line 36 inches up from the bottom edge.

A good way to be sure you have a consistent measurement of 36 inches is to use a yardstick to make marks in several places. Then line up another sheet of 8-foot by 4-foot ⅝-inch board to link up all of the marks you've made, forming one continuous horizontal line (see Figure 1).

Now you are about to mark your curve-riding slope. The easiest way to do this is to get some sturdy rope that doesn't stretch. Place a peg in a spot in the ground 9 feet straight forward from the bottom corner of the plywood (see Figure 2).

Tie a dark-leaded pencil, carpenter's crayon, or Magic Marker to the other end of the string. Be sure to keep the

distance from peg to marker at 9 feet. Have a friend hold down the peg before you make your mark in order to keep the string taut and peg grounded.

The idea now is to swing the marker from the peg pivot point so that it traces a curved slope along your plywood surface. Mark that line, being sure to intersect with the line you've made 36 inches up from the bottom.

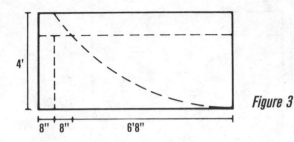

Figure 3

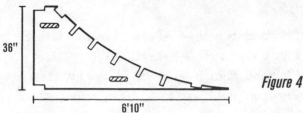

Figure 4

The top flat surface of the ramp, as you can now see, it is too wide; you want to trim it down. So mark a line 8 inches in from the left edge (see Figure 3). At this point, you've got the basic shape of all of the uprights.

Cut off all of the excess wood you've marked. You'll probably want to use a circular saw to lop off huge chunks and then a scroll saw to cut the perfect curved line.

You have a model, or template, now. Use this piece to mark and cut the remaining three pieces of 8-foot by 4-foot ⅝-inch plywood.

Step 2: Cutting Interior Uprights

Two of your uprights will form the outer edges of the ramp, and two will form an interior supporting structure for two-by-four cross-pieces.

You will be cutting the interior uprights now, making space to hold and support your two-by-fours. To get an idea of why you are cutting these holes, glance ahead to illustrations showing the interior of the ramp.

Now we will make cutouts for the boxlike structure

behind the upper end of the ramp. Cut rectangular notches (widest horizontally) to match the actual measurements of your two-by-fours (see Figure 4). Remember that most so-called two-by-fours are more like 1⅝ inches by 3¾ inches—but do measure the ones you've got.

Okay, you've accounted for the boxlike structure. We're moving on to marking notches for your cross-pieces. These two-by-fours support the weight of riders and skates so that your plywood structure doesn't bow or collapse.

Step 3: Joining Exterior and Interior Templates

Now you want to join sets of interior and exterior templates to form mirror-opposite pairs. Two-by-fours will rest in the notches of the interior templates (see Figure 5).

Line up your templates. Make sure you understand exactly what you are doing before you nail! The interior templates must face each other. Line up your templates, making sure you can envision the finished look and where the lumber will finally be attached. Now join interior and exterior templates with nails or screws.

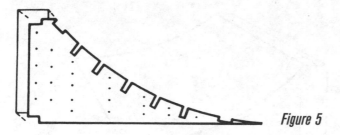

Figure 5

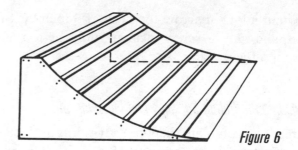

Figure 6

Step 4: Cutting and Attaching Cross-Running Supports

Now provide supports for your structure. These will be two-by-fours. Each should be 3 feet, 10¾ inches in length. Make nine of them.

Step 5: Building Your Structural Frame

Attach your two-by-fours to the templates by driving nails or screws through from the outside of the exterior templates into the butt-ends of the cross-pieces. Be sure your two-by-fours rest securely and neatly into the interior template notches. Remember that seven of your cross-pieces will be on the curved slope, one at the top back, and another at the bottom back (see Figure 6).

Step 6: Adding Diagonal Braces and a Small Top Deck

Your boxlike structure is still susceptible to side-to-side wobble. With all of the abuse you'll be giving it, you need internal bracing. That's why it's important to add diagonal internal supports.

These supports need to be measured, based on the exact measurements of your jump ramp as it now stands. The ends of your two-by-fours should rest flush on the top and bottom of the inside of the box at the back of your jump ramp. (That's why they should be angle-cut.) Once cut, drive them into place with nails or screws, forming an X-like shape behind your box (see Figure 7).

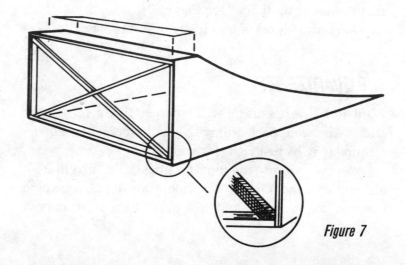

Figure 7

Now cut a long, narrow top deck of 8-inch by 4-foot plywood, and nail or screw it down onto the top of the boxlike end of your ramp.

Step 7: Adding the Riding Surfaces and Finishing Off!

You're ready to complete the job. Your riding surface will have two layers—a bottom one of ⅜-inch plywood for support and a top one of ¼-inch plywood that you'll actually roll on.

To measure the exact dimensions of your support surface, use a tape measure to gauge the curved distance of your slope from top to bottom. Cut and join it to your curved slope. Start at the top, and proceed downward. Be sure to drive nails into two-by-fours, not into air!

Now do the same with your ¼-inch plywood riding surface. Finally, coat the entire structure with several layers of outdoor urethane (see Figure 8).

Congratulations, you're ready to jump!

THE QUARTER-PIPE

Want to try vert skating without spending a fortune or dominating your backyard with a half-pipe? Then a quarter-pipe may be just right for you.

You can sail into the pipe, fly up its side, turn in mid-air, and descend. Or you can ride toward a quarter-pipe from an oblique angle and do a quick turn on its curved

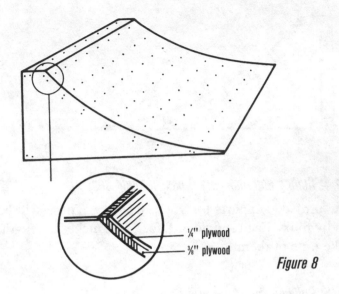

¼" plywood
⅜" plywood

Figure 8

surface. You can also use your quarter-pipe to explore wall-riding maneuvers.

Unlike a launch ramp, a quarter-pipe does not send you forward beyond it in the same direction you were going. Instead, it can propel you flying into the blue yonder above or onto a wall.

The design of this particular quarter-pipe does not allow for lip tricks (moves done riding the upper edge). There is no upper platform to catch you, the way there is on a huge half-pipe. Save lip trickery for cruises on the big monster. Or, consider adding an upper landing and railing to this quarter-pipe's design.

Materials

- Plywood, ½-inch or ⅝-inch—2 sheets, 4 feet by 8 feet
- Plywood, ¼-inch—2 sheets, 4 feet by 8 feet
- Two-by-fours—10 pieces, each 4 feet long
- Two-by-fours—2 pieces, each 5 feet, 9 inches long
- Nails
- Hammer
- Cross saw
- Circular saw
- Scroll saw
- Drill—hand or power

Step 1: Cut Wood for Upright Supports

Begin by cutting both of your ½- or ⅝-inch-thick sheets of plywood into two equal-size squares, each 4 feet by 4 feet (see Figure 9).

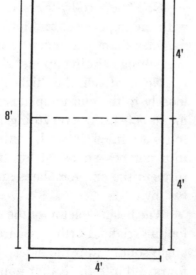

Figure 9

Step 2: Mark Curved Cut-Lines

You are going to swing a pencil from a pivot point to demark a curved cutting line. Begin by hammering a nail into any corner. Tie a 4-foot-long string with a pencil on it to that nail. Swing the string, keeping it taut, and mark your cutting line. The shape you've marked should taper to a thin edge as it reaches two side corners (see Figure 10).

To make your second support, simply remove the nail and place it in the wood at the farthest, opposite corner of the square. Swing the rope again and make your second template cutting line.

Finally, cut your third template from the remaining square. This will leave you with some scrap lumber, since you need only three uprights for this project.

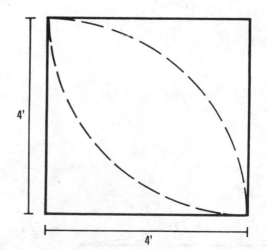

Figure 10

Step 3: Make an Interior Upright

This support holds up the middle surface of your ramp. Because it will hold two-by-fours that run across it, we need to recess those two-by-fours by cutting notches for them.

Mark notch holes equal to the true height and width of your two-by-fours (which are never exactly 2 inches high by 4 inches wide). Make eight notches 6 inches apart. Close to both tapered edges of your template, the wood becomes too narrow to allow a deep notch to be cut. Assume that the two-by-four in this slot will lie on its wide side, and cut a notch to fit (see Figure 11).

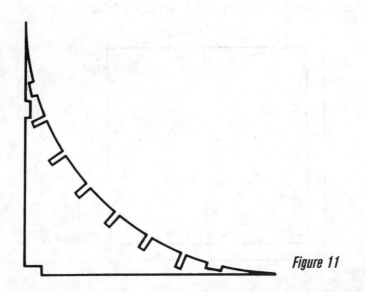

Figure 11

Step 4: Cut Hand Holes for Carrying

Your quarter-pipe should be easy for two people to carry, each using two hands. Make life easy for yourself and your friends by cutting oval hand holes about 5 inches across in two positions on each of the end templates.

Drill a wide hole in the center of the shapes you've marked for your hand holes. This will make it easy to get your cross saw blade into the wood to do the cutting.

Step 5: Assemble the Skeleton of Your Quarter-Pipe

Work with a friend on this part of the job. First, fit your four-foot long two-by-fours into the central template's notches.

Nail the two-by-fours loosely into place, beginning with the uppermost and lowest ones. You don't want to hammer them permanently into place until you're sure everything is lining up just right.

Now, attach the highest and lowest two-by-fours loosely to the end templates. You're still making adjustments, ensuring everything fits well. Once the two-by-fours are lined up well, continue inserting two-by-fours into notches and securing them with nails hammered through the end templates and into the butt-ends of the two-by-fours.

The basic skeleton of the ramp should now be up and looking right. Further secure it by driving nails at an angle solidly into the sides of all cross-running two-by-fours and into the center uplift.

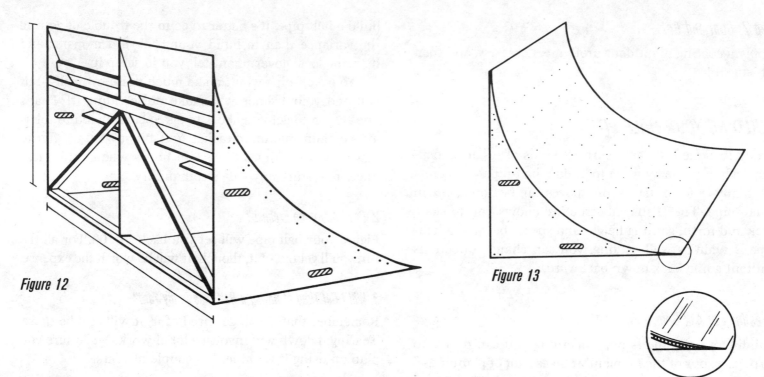

Figure 12

Figure 13

Don't let nail heads protrude onto the area where you'll be nailing your skating surface.

To give extra support to the rear boxlike structure of the ramp, nail 5-foot, 9-inch two-by-fours on the diagonal as shown in Figure 12.

Step 6: Apply the Surface Plywood

Your skating surface will be two layers of the ¼-inch thick plywood. Begin at what will be the upper end of your ramp. Nail the plywood into all three uprights, plus every two-by-four that runs under it. Repeat the process with a second layer of plywood surface.

To give yourself a smooth cruise when riding up your ramp, be sure the surface meets the ground evenly. Accomplish this by tapering the bottom layers with a power saw. See Figure 13 for the edge you want.

Step 7: Coat and Go!

Apply a coating of outdoor urethane. Let it dry, and then let 'em rip!

BUILDING YOUR HALF-PIPE

Ready to skate high and learn all kinds of in-air maneuvers? Then you may want to build a half-pipe.

Many kinds of tricks and moves can be done *only* on a half-pipe. The U-shaped structure allows you to skate back and forth, gaining height and speed. Because a half-pipe is wide as well as long, you can change directions without going back down backward.

Questions to Ask Before Building

Building a half-pipe is not something you can decide to do on the spur of the moment. It takes a lot of planning—as well as a lot of hard work and money.

1. Where Am I Going to Build It?

Because your structure will occupy a considerable amount of real estate, you want to obtain permission first. Teens, allow me to state the obvious: Don't build it as a surprise Mother's Day present! (Or as a gift for yourself without parents' permission.)

Perhaps more important than parental approval is legal approval and, where appropriate, your neighbors' permission. You will probably need a zoning variance to build a half-pipe. It's better to go to the trouble of getting the variance than to build your backyard monster and have the local government tell you to scrap it.

Your half-pipe won't make much noise by itself—but you and your friends will make noise riding it! That's one reason to get neighbors to agree beforehand to tolerate a certain amount of racket. You might want to offer to restrict skating times to certain hours when you're less likely to disturb anybody's tranquillity.

2. Can I Afford the Expense?

Figure your half-pipe will set you back $1,500. For all the fun you'll get out of it, though, it will be worth the expense.

3. Will I Get Tired of Having a Half-Pipe in my Yard?

Remember that if you get tired of it, it will still be there. Tearing it down will involve a lot of work. Make sure you plan on using it for at least a couple of years.

Terminology

Before we start building it, let's clarify some useful terms:

- *Drop-in chute or channel.* Used in some half-pipe designs, this is a notch in the landing/vert juncture with a curved surface that allows a skater to drop into the ramp without going over a lip. Because experienced lip tricksters enjoy riding the uninterrupted length of the lip, our ramp plan excludes a drop-in chute.

- *Flat.* The bottom, horizontal riding surface.
- *Lip.* A rounded edge where your landing and vert meet. This is usually made of PVC pipe, which gives a smooth ride and prevents wear on the lumber.
- *Roll-out deck.* A landing on the upper edges of a half-pipe. A skater can begin on a landing or ride up to it.
- *Transition.* The angled riding surface of a half-pipe or quarter-pipe.
- *Vert.* Vertical skating surface. This is the portion of the riding slope of any pipe or wall that is vertical or mostly so.

Materials

- Plywood, ⅜ inch — 100 sheets, 4 feet by 8 feet. These will be both your riding surface and internal/external supports.
- Garden timbers or four-by-fours — 56 lengths. Use them to make your base frame.
- Two-by-fours — 70 (16-foot) lengths. Your inner cross-beams and reinforcement lumber will come from these.
- PVC pipe, 2 inch — 2 (16-foot) lengths. You will slice this pipe down the middle to form lip edges.
- Nails or screws — Nails go in more easily. Worth considering: screws come out more easily, should you ever dismantle your half-pipe.

- Hammer
- Cross saw
- Scroll saw
- Circular saw
- Outdoor urethane — For coating and weather-proofing the structure.

Step 1: Build the Foundation

As they say, a house is only as good as its foundation. Make yours strong, evenly laid and level, and as close to perfectly rectangular as you can get (see Figure 14).

Make sure your flat structure of garden timbers or four-by-fours rests on level ground. If you're building on dirt or grass, remove clumps and high spots; fill in holes and depressions. Asphalt can be imperfect, too. When you're reasonably convinced that your surface is flat, lay

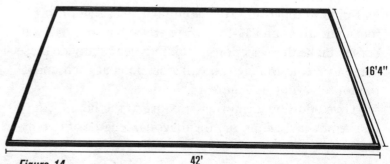

Figure 14

16'4"

42'

your timbers without nailing them together. Use pieces of wood (shims) to make sure all is level, checking with a carpenter's level.

Make your foundation 42 feet long and 16 feet, 4 inches wide. Finally, join the timbers together to make a giant rectangle by driving nails in them at an angle. Drive the nails in on the sides. Use the tops only if you are sure you can sink the nail heads completely below the surface of the wood.

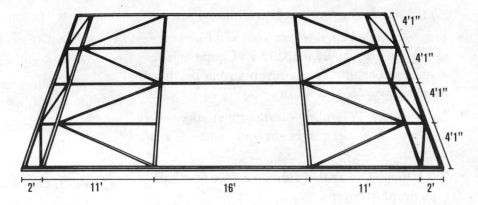

Figure 15

Step 2: Reinforce the Frame

Begin by placing a 42-foot-long run of timbers down the middle of the horizontal length of the structure.

Your goal now is to create extra bottom support for the deck, transitional, and vertical areas, which will carry most of the structure's overall weight. Now we want to create eight boxlike frames on each end of the half-pipe foundation. To accomplish this, section off 2-foot-wide areas and 11-foot-wide areas. Lay and nail timbers to make these sections solid. Further subdivide these areas to create the eight boxlike sections at each end of the foundation (see Figure 15).

Give additional internal support to the boxes you've marked by laying and nailing diagonal lengths of two-by-fours.

Step 3: Construct Your Upright Templates

These uprights provide the large vertical skeleton on which your half-pipe rests. Each upright sits on a length of timber. Your goal at the beginning will be to construct a template, which you can use to trace cut-lines for all other upright supports.

You will be building four exterior and six interior uprights.

Exterior uprights are the ones you can see when you look at the half-pipe from the side. They *don't* have notches in them, because the riding surface gets nailed directly into their edges.

Interior uprights eventually get hidden within the structure. These *do* have notches for receiving cross-running two-by-fours.

Begin with a 4-foot by 8-foot sheet of ⅜-inch plywood. Now cut a rectangular notch in the lower end of one corner of the sheet. Make that notch 1 foot, 6 inches high by 1 foot wide (see Figure 16). Now lay one sheet of plywood horizontally below and fitting into the notched piece, forming an L-shaped structure (see Figure 17).

At this point, you're ready to mark the curved line that will form the slope of your transitional and vertical areas.

To mark the curved line, you will use a radius formed by a 9-foot-long two-by-four

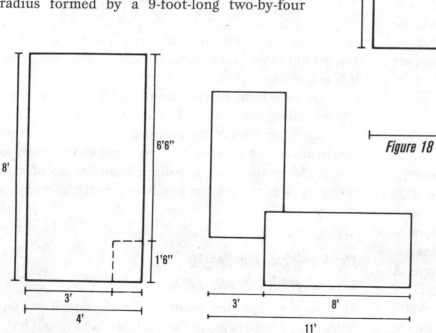

Figure 16

Figure 17

Figure 18

attached on one end with a large nail at the pivot point and to a marker pencil at the other end.

Position the two-by-four radius at a spot exactly 9 feet, 3¾ inches in a vertical line above the edge of the lower piece of plywood (see Figure 18). Now swing the two-by-four so that it marks a curved line that stops at the bottom at 3⅜ inches from the bottom edge of the plywood.

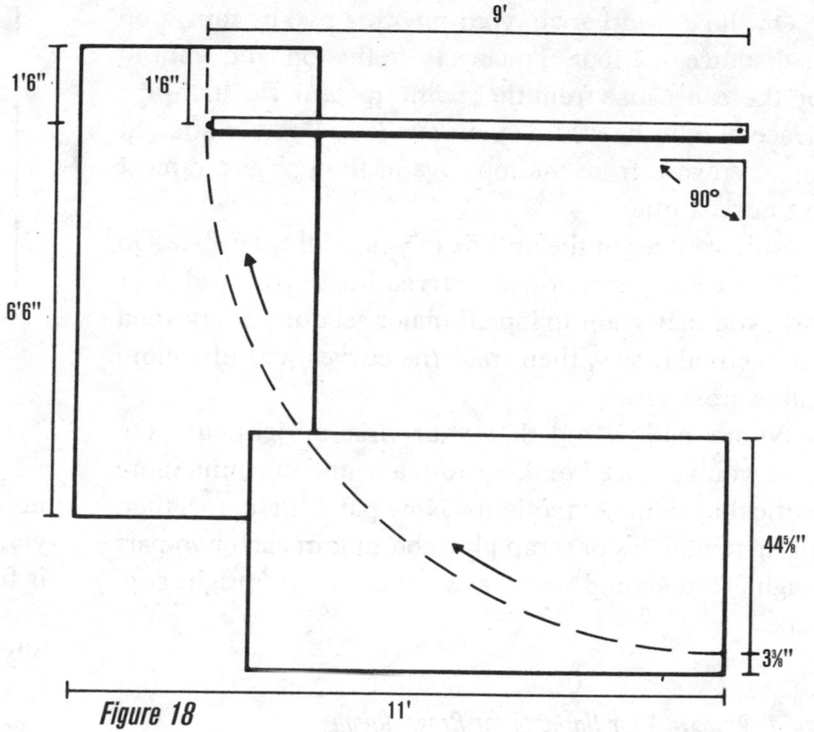

On the upward arc of your pivoting two-by-four, stop at a distance of 1 foot, 6 inches from the top. You want to stop there, because from that point upward, the half-pipe surface should be 100 percent vertical. Draw a straight line downward from the top edge of the upright to meet your curved line.

Now you've got the outline of your riding surface. Go cut! Use a scroll saw for the curved lines. To speed your work, you may want to lop off major sections of plywood with a circular saw, then trace the curves with the more nimble cross saw.

Before nailing together your first upright, use the pieces you've traced and cut to mark and cut nine more identical upright components. Now patch them together, nailing rectangles of scrap plywood to join each two-part upright. You should now have a total of 10 upright supports.

Step 4: Prepare Your Uprights for Cross-Beams

The cross-beams of your structure don't rest on top of the edges of your plywood—they're recessed *into* them. This gives your entire structure more internal strength all around.

Mark and cut notches in the bottom-most sections of your uprights. These notches should be placed sideways. That's because your uprights are narrow down there. A long notch would cut the bottom of your upright off.

Make four of these sideways notches, each the width and height of your two-by-fours. (Remember that two-by-fours are not exactly 2 inches by 4 inches!) Space your

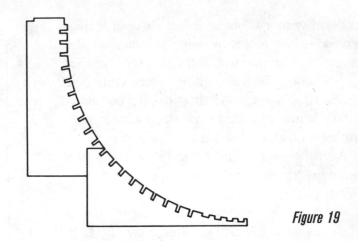

Figure 19

notches six inches apart on your transitional area. When you get to the vertical section, 8 inches between notches is fine (see Figure 19).

Important Note: Keep in mind that you will eventually be nailing horizontally laid sheets of plywood 4 feet in width. The edges of the plywood must be driven into two-by-fours, not into the air. So eyeball and measure as you go. Make sure that, beginning from the top of your riding surface, every 4 feet you have a notch to receive a two-by-four.

Step 5: Reinforce Your Uprights with L-Shaped Two-by-Four Braces

To give your uprights greater strength, attach two-by-fours to the outer edges of the uprights. Nail through the plywood into the two-by-fours.

Place the two-by-four that reinforces the vertical edge of plywood on one side of that plywood. The bottom-running two-by-four should be on the opposite side. This is important in terms of joining the 2 two-by-fours to form a solid L (see Figure 20).

Now create L-shaped braces for all of your remaining uprights (a total of four exterior and six interior).

This part is a lot of work, but you and your friends are no doubt up to the challenge! To keep up your energy levels, remember that your half-pipe will be only as good as its internal structure. Make it strong, and you'll ride long.

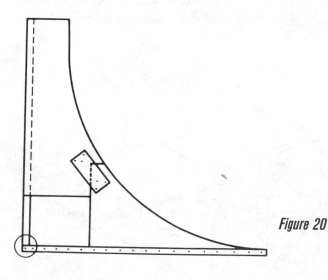

Figure 20

Step 6: Raise Your Uprights

Similar to an old-fashioned community activity like a barn-raising, this should be a thrilling joint activity for you and your soon-to-be airborne pals.

Before nailing your uprights into place, double-check your measurements. You don't want to nail any plywood riding surface into air. If something is off, you can attach strips of two-by-fours to your timbers to extend them, width-wise, enabling them to receive nails at the right place.

Pay special care to your 16-foot length of future flat riding surface, the bottom of the ramp. Start at the exact center point of the ramp and make sure your 8-foot sections of plywood will all rest on timbers near their ends.

It's just about essential to have a bunch of skaters to assist you now. Put up two exterior uprights. Get them to stand up by running and nailing a 16-foot two-by-four across the back edges of the ends of the uprights (see Figure 21). Don't attach this 16-foot length too firmly, because you'll be removing it shortly.

Have one person hold up this 16-foot board, to keep the structure from collapsing. Then nail the exterior uprights into the bottom timbers with diagonally driven nails.

Position the interior uprights now, and line them up accurately. Temporarily attach the back edges of these to your 16-footer, too. Look at your structure now from several directions, making sure it looks straight and vertical. Do the interior uprights look good? Then nail them into place at the bottom.

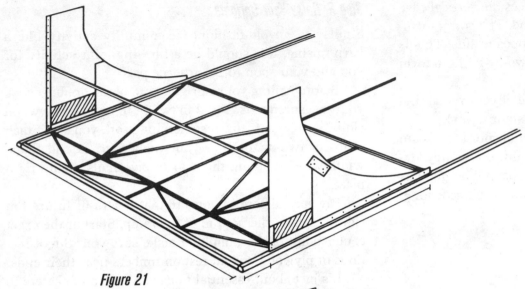

Figure 21

between your exterior flat area timbers. That's why we'll build a short lip along the outer timbers—to give you something to butt your cross-pieces against. Make this lip by positioning and nailing two-by-fours atop the outer timber (see Figure 23). Keep the narrow edge of the two-by-four facing upward.

Be certain that the distance between one inside edge of this lip and the other across the flatland is 16 feet.

It's time to further strengthen the structure with two-by-four cross-pieces (see Figure 22), otherwise it could still collapse like a flimsy parallelogram. You've built the internal structure for one-half of your half-pipe—now repeat the process and build the other end.

Step 7: Building Flatland!

You will be running horizontal lengths of supporting two-by-fours

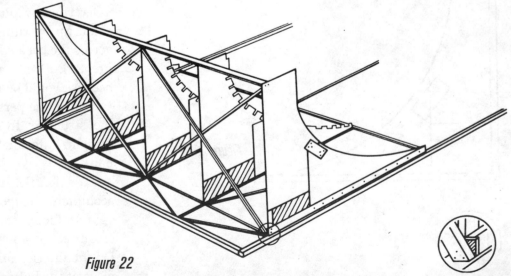

Figure 22

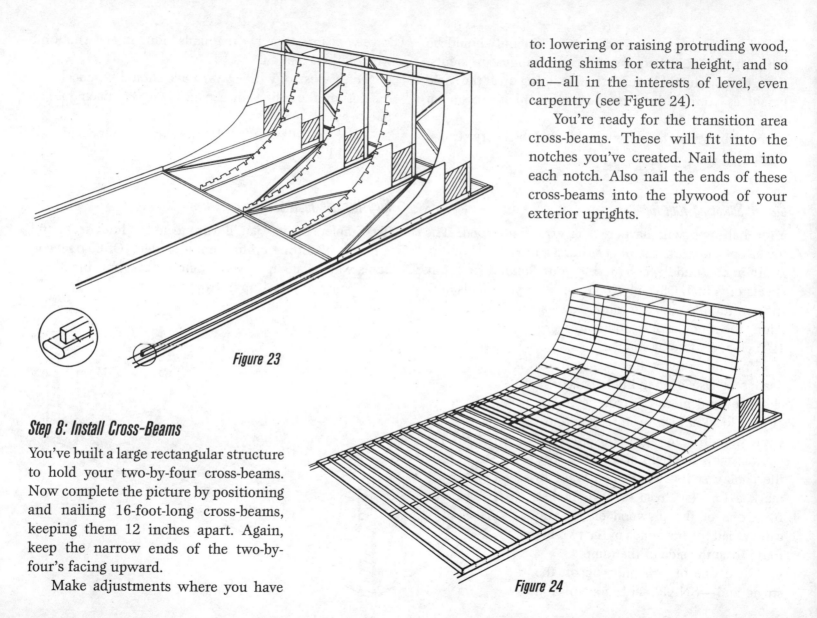

Figure 23

to: lowering or raising protruding wood, adding shims for extra height, and so on—all in the interests of level, even carpentry (see Figure 24).

You're ready for the transition area cross-beams. These will fit into the notches you've created. Nail them into each notch. Also nail the ends of these cross-beams into the plywood of your exterior uprights.

Step 8: Install Cross-Beams

You've built a large rectangular structure to hold your two-by-four cross-beams. Now complete the picture by positioning and nailing 16-foot-long cross-beams, keeping them 12 inches apart. Again, keep the narrow ends of the two-by-four's facing upward.

Make adjustments where you have

Figure 24

The cross-beams closest to your flatland should be lying on their side. Because of our design measurements, though, they should have no trouble lining up at the same height as your flatland cross-beams, which are up on their narrow edges.

Your backyard behemoth suddenly looks very strong, doesn't it?

Step 9: Surfacing Your Ramp

Your half-pipe will have two layers of plywood. The lower one supports the upper riding surface. To build it: Begin at the middle, conquering your flatland first. Lay sheets of ⅜-inch CDX plywood. Drive in your nails at 6-inch intervals on the outer edges. Along the inner surface, nail into every 12-inch-apart two-by-four below.

How do you hit the two-by-fours dead on? Use a snap-line! This is a chalk-covered piece of string. Get one at your local hardware store. You'll use your snap-line to mark off lines on boards, with the help of a friend. Lay the chalky string where you want to mark a line (such as every 6 inches from one of the plywood ends). You can eyeball the butt-ends of the two-by-fours from the side of the ramp.

Then one of you pulls up on the string and—SNAP!—it's a snap! You have your line. Simply drive nails along it, and you'll hit wood rather than air.

For a sense of where your nails should be, check out the dots on the riding surface on Figure 25. Each dot is a nail-head!

Once you've installed the first layer of plywood, add a second layer.

Step 10: Late Touches

To complete the job, you'll want to add roll-out decks and a means of getting up to them—ladders. Of course, you can always skate up to your roll-out deck, but sometimes you'll want to just drop in from the top.

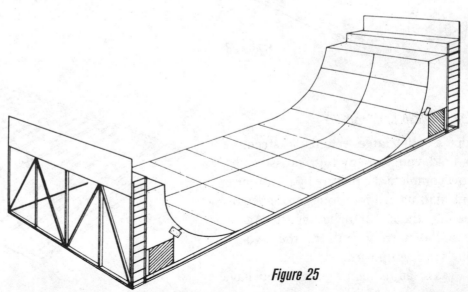

Figure 25

Before putting up your top decks, run short widths of two-by-fours in the open rectangular area where they'll sit. Then nail plywood rectangles into place. Add a fence at the top back that you'll also make out of plywood. This will keep unwary skaters from falling off.

Buy a couple of wood ladders to help you get up to the top, and screw them into place at the top, using hinges.

Step 11: Give Yourself Some Lip

You'll want to experiment with some lip tricks—moves where you slide along the joint where your roll-out deck and vert meet. To make that easier to do, you add PVC piping. It allows you to roll smoothly.

Buy two pieces of 16-foot, 2-inch-thick piping, and using a circular saw, cut them lengthwise, removing one-quarter (a 90-degree arc) of each. This will give you two 270-degree sections, each 16 feet long. You'll attach this piping with deck screws. But you want to be sure the screw heads are well recessed. So counter-sink them.

Now screw the piping into the upper decks, making sure they rest flush against the wood where they meet your vert section.

Step 12: Preserving Your Masterpiece

You're not done yet. Now coat this beauty with outdoor polyurethane. Sure it costs a lot, but you've got many hours tied up in this masterpiece. A word about foul weather treatment, if you're in a northern climate: When winter approaches, keep snow and ice off your ramp with strong, heavy tarpaulins.

Wow, you did it! You built the most colossal fun center known to skaters. Along the way, you've become a skilled carpenter. Go skate!

14

SKATEFLECTIONS

*T*rying to pin down a permanent picture of in-line skating is like attempting to pick up quicksilver. The more we try to hold on to it, the more the sport eludes our grasp.

This changeability is part of its beauty! Skaters continually invent—devise new moves, improved equipment, and innovative ways of having fun.

Skating is fluid grace—people empowered to move. That movement is in synchrony with the world; it's an expression of the self in harmonious artistry. Or skating can be opposed to the world as it

195

exists. Try telling the aggressive streetstyle skater that his moves are at one with the universe. He'd say it's a hoax! Attitude is all.

The future will reveal new attitudes—intriguing, more rewarding ways of rolling. Allow me to predict for a moment.

So take this not as an oil painting of the future, but rather as a misty view through the sorceress's globe. . . .

I predict skaters rolling to and from work regularly. They'll be so common that you won't even notice them. In fact, you could well be one of them. Skating will also be more aromatic—I predict that employers, skaters themselves, will provide showers at work for everyone.

In the future, in-line dance will become a popular art form. Men and women will delight in the beauty they can create on a set of wheels. The fact that skating can be done almost anywhere will give figure skating and dancing a universality far beyond that achieved by ice skating.

In-line hockey will grow into an even greater super sport, involving more young people than even baseball and soccer. It's fast, it's fun, it's relatively safe. For every dad, mom, and tyke—"What's not to like?"

Racing on in-line skates will continue to captivate and entertain—building interest and zeal, even among the left-behinds. Inspired, they will then try skating—and find they love it!

Stick around. The future of in-line skating knows no bounds.

APPENDIX A

NATIONAL ASSOCIATIONS AND ORGANIZATIONS

GENERAL IN-LINE SKATING ORGANIZATIONS

International In-Line Skating Association (IISA)

P.O. Box 15482

Atlanta, GA 30333

Tel: 404-728-9707

The IISA certifies instructors and is a good contact for the name of an instructor in your area. IISA publishes guidelines on in-line hockey and speed skating. In the works are guidelines for extreme skating, which includes ramps, vert, jumps, and stair riding.

United States Amateur Confederation of Roller Skating (USAC/RS)

P.O. Box 6579

Lincoln, NE 68506

Tel: 402-483-7551

SPEED-SKATING ORGANIZATIONS

Amateur Speedskating Union of the United States(ASU)

National Office

1033 Shady Lane

Glen Ellyn, IL 60136

Tel: 800-634-4766

   708-790-3230

Ontario Speed Skating Association

1220 Sheppard Avenue East

Willowdale, Ontario

Canada M2K 2X1

Tel: 416-495-4043

Fax: 416-495-4329

IN-LINE HOCKEY ORGANIZATIONS

Amateur In-Line Hockey

National In-Line Hockey Association (NIHA)

1221 Brickell Avenue

9th Floor

Miami, FL 33131

Tel: 800-358-NIHA (members only)

   305-358-8988 (head office)

Fax: 305-374-4754 (members' fax)

   305-358-8846 (administration fax)

NIHA promotes and sanctions in-line leagues and
teams. It also provides insurance, rulebooks and
other literature, and videotapes. Contact NIHA for
help in starting a club or league or for any other
question related to in-line hockey. (For more details,
see Chapter 10.)

United States Amateur Confederation of Roller Skating (USAC/RS)

P.O. Box 6579

Lincoln, NE 68506

Tel: 402-483-7551

USAC/RS promotes and sanctions in-line leagues and
teams, organized into five distinct categories. It also
provides insurance, rule books and other literature,
and videotapes. Contact USAC/RS for help in
starting a club or league, or for any other questions
related to in-line hockey. (For more details, see
Chapter 10.)

Professional In-Line Hockey

RHI

Roller-Hockey International

5182 Katella #106

Los Alamitos, CA 90720

LOCAL CLUBS AND ORGANIZATIONS

The following list of local clubs has been provided by InLine magazine. (For a subscription to InLine, call 800-877-5281.) InLine notes that the club listings are constantly changing. They invite you to write to the magazine for an updated list of in-line clubs and events throughout the country. Write to: Information Request, InLine, 2025 Pearl Street, Boulder, CO 80302; telephone 303-440-5111. Please include a stamped, self-addressed envelope and allow four weeks for delivery.

Local General In-Line Skating Clubs

Arizona

Valley In-Line, Ray Pisar, 602-831-2166, Tempe, Arizona—Skates once a week in different parts of the valley area. Location and times vary weekly. IISA instructors available for lessons.

California

Bay Area In-Line Racers, Lee Cole, 415-244-9800, San Francisco, California—Focus is on setting up races. Members participate in about two to four races per year.

Central Coast Rollers, Jim Petrik, W: 805-237-8766, H: 805-466-7109, Paso Robles, California—Informal recreational club.

El Dorado In-Line Skating Assn., Scott Johnson, 916-672-3124/916-622-5809, El Dorado, California.

Golden Gate Skate Patrol, David Miles, 415-752-1967, San Francisco, California—The Midnight Rollers skate Friday nights at 8 p.m.

Humbolt In-Line Skate Club, Don Hoch, 707-826-1769, Arcata, California—Putting together clinics and an in-line hockey program.

In-Line Rollerworks, Kon Ammosow, 714-675-6772, Costa Mesa, California—A ramp and in-line club. Putting together some events.

Nor-Cal Skeelers, Flying Wheels Speed Club, Rick Babington, W: 209-521-6816, H: 209-524-7928, Modesto, California—An indoor and outdoor club that holds a variety of fund-raisers, competitions, and races.

Sacramento In-Line Skate Assn., Mel Ryan-Roberts, W: 916-443-2527, H: 916-962-2762, Sacramento, California—Trying to get bike trail along river open to skaters.

Santa Rosa In-Line Skate Club, Chartelle Tarrant, 707-538-2823, Santa Rosa, California—Full men's skate. Occasionally, groups go to San Francisco at night. Sunday skates held two times a month (community and long distance). Putting together a women's roller hockey team.

Silver Streaks, Layne Hacket, 408-354-5605, Los Gatos, California—Winter: skate twice a week. Summer: skate three times a week. Other activities include skate trips, video analysis to check progress, and occasional social events.

Team Karim, Adlai Karim, 510-849-4004,
Fax: 510-841-2181, Berkeley, California—Speed
teams for in-line and ice. Skaters can come and
workout during team practices.

Whistler Wheels In-Line Skate Club, Simon Hudson,
604-932-7201, Whistler, British Columbia, Canada—
Four skating levels: club participant, club skater,
recreational competitive skater, and team
competitive skater. Includes coaching for freestyle,
hockey, racing, and skate-to-ski disciplines. IISA-
certified instructors available.

Colorado

Rocky Mountain Skating Club/Storm, Ginger
Conrad, W: 303-290-6505, Fax: 303-290-0638,
Littleton, Colorado—Storm: sponsored by RISK and
Grand West Outfitters. For extreme skaters only.

Connecticut

Team High Gear, Chris Pollard, 704-537-5064,
Stamford, Connecticut, and Charlotte, North
Carolina—In-line racing team that has events in
both Stamford and Charlotte. Sponsored by Miller
Brewing Company.

District of Columbia

Washington Area Rollerskaters, John Vanderwolf, 202-
466-5005, Washington, D.C.—Meets four times a week
for recreational skating. Holds trail skates, occasional
biweekly races in summer, and other events.

Florida

Beach Bladers of South Florida, Tom Baker,
407-495-8326, Del Ray Beach, Florida—Educates
club members on safety. Holds weekly
"Fundamental & Freestyle" clinics. Open to all ages.

Central Florida Lightning, Wheels of Florida, 407-
869-9652, Orlando, Florida—Strictly speed skating.
Skate two or three times per week. Skate indoors at
Semeron Skateway and outdoors at Glen Ridge
Middle School and the quadrangle at UCF.

Hollywood Beach Skating Assn., Michael
Martocchio, 305-927-0100, Hollywood, Florida—
Recently formed in-line skating club that promotes
family fun and safe skating on the boardwalk at
Hollywood Beach. Meets Wednesdays at 7:30 p.m. at
the pavilion on Garfield Street.

New River Rollers, George Batchelor, 305-963-2653,
Ft. Lauderdale, Florida—A social, nonprofit group.
Holds fund-raisers. Meets Tuesday and Thursday
evenings. Skates through Ft. Lauderdale. Beginners
to advanced and speed skaters.

SOBE Rollers, Eric Kraftsau, 305-672-5786, Fisher
Island, Florida—Meets Mondays at South Beach for
a 4-mile skate along the beach and through parks,
plus a post-skate party. Sportsman Paradise will be
giving free rentals to skaters in order to increase
membership.

St. Augustine Skating Assn., Kent Bowers,
904-797-4772, St. Augustine, Florida—Trying to

form a club. Needs members! Plans to have a group skate once a week and morning workouts.

Trailways and Pinellas Trail Skate, Tom Selhorst, 813-461-9736, Clearwater, Florida—Skate on the Pinellas trail (47 miles long, open to bikes and skates only). From pro-level racing to recreational skating. Heavy training for pros on Sundays and 30 miles of recreational skating on Saturdays at 1 p.m. Open to all ages.

Illinois

Chicago Land Bladers, Randy McManigal, 708-597-5686, Orland Park, Illinois—Promotes safety. Raises funds for good causes and "has a lot of fun." Group skates once a week on trails by lakefront. All ranges of ages and skills.

Jacksonville In-liners, George Jaworski, 217-243-4427, Jacksonville, Illinois.

Rainbow Rollers, Milan Metrovic, 312-775-4681, Chicago, Illinois—Open to all ages and skills (including stunt skaters, racers, and recreational skaters). Focus is shifting from racing to recreation. Planning a hockey team. Group skates three to four times per week. Competition team: Team Rainbow.

Indiana

Indy In-Liners, Terry Sullivan, 317-574-CLUB, Indianapolis, Indiana—Members include racers, freestyle skaters, and hockey players (a league).

Group skates Sunday mornings in downtown Indianapolis and in the Rollerdome at the Hoosier Dome in the winters.

Iowa

River City Rollers, Dan Martin, 712-252-2445, Sioux City, Iowa—Skates led by a certified skating instructor every Wednesday night. Focus is on long-distance skating.

Maryland

Baltimore Street Skaters Club, Hal Ashman, 410-666-9463, Timonium, Maryland—Meets on first and third Thursday of month from 7 to 9 p.m. in a Timonium parking lot. Clinic situation: 45-min. to 1-hour lesson, then free skate. Skate at Gunpowder State Park, Lochraven Reservoir, and Camden Yards.

Massachusetts

In-Line Club of Boston (ICB), Damon Poole, 617-932-5457, Boston, Massachusetts—Holds races, half-pipe, and noncompetitive events. Also offers free clinics, retail discounts, newsletter, hotline, and more.

Michigan

City Rollers, Mark Farnen, 313-824-0011, Grosse Point Park, Michigan—Indoor skates once per week in the winter and outdoor skates five days per week in the summer. Includes recreational and stunt skating, racing, and hockey. Takes many trips and has developed a national-affiliation club.

Straights and Eights, Dave Cooper, 313-568-9889, Dearborn, Michigan—The oldest outdoor skating club in Michigan. Holds Monday-night meetings and in-line fitness courses and supplies IISA-certified instruction. Individual instruction, family and group touring, and in-line destination vacations are made available.

Team Extreme, Frank Fedel, 313-292-6283, Dearborn Heights, Michigan—An outdoor racing club that meets at the Pontiac Silver Dome once a week for indoor skating during the winter.

Wolverine Speed Skating Club, Bob Sklar, 313-855-4267, Farmington Hills, Michigan.

Minnesota

MN Dive Center In-Line Skating Assn., Jim Campos, 507-288-8802, Rochester, Minnesota—Meets every other Thursday and one Sunday per month for a night skate. The club offers lessons and sets up special events.

Northern In-Line Skaters, Joe Maki, 218-722-0106, Duluth, Minnesota—Meets on Tuesday and Sunday mornings for recreational skating. Meets Thursdays for race training.

Missouri

In-Line Club of Kansas City (ICKC), Kevin Dillard, 816-590-8598, Kansas City, Missouri—Activities include group skates, roller hockey, skate instruction, clinics, races, freestyle, and occasional social events.

New Hampshire

Granite State Skate Club, Deborah Huntley, 603-886-5802, Nashua, New Hampshire—A new, recreational club focusing on skill improvement and safety.

New Jersey

New Jersey Skate Club, Linda Lines, 908-244-2483, Toms River, New Jersey—Indoor/outdoor group skates two or three times a week. Getting into racing. Adults only.

New Mexico

Mountains and Rivers Skate Club, Tim Cone, 505-268-4876, Albuquerque, New Mexico—An informal association. Hockey Monday nights 7:30–12. Group skates on Tucsdays. Beginners' clinics on Sunday at 9 a.m.

New York

Groove Skate Club, Gina Tonzi, 315-437-5124, Syracuse, New York—Club includes clinics; a slalom dryland program; and morning, night, and group skates.

In-Line Groove, John Ghidiu, 315-625-5145, Syracuse, New York—Has evening skates, training programs, hip-hop skating, technical seminar, discounts, and instruction.

Long Island Road And Track Skating Assn., Don Phillips, 516-868-2160, Freeport, New York— Meets four times a week (mid-spring through mid-October) at "Cedar Creek Park" in Wantagh. Holds Wednesday night parties at the rink, Friday night introduction to in-line racing, Saturday night outdoor skates, and Sunday afternoon free clinics.

New York Road Skaters Assn., Priscilla Boehme, 212-534-7858, New York, New York—Club includes events, night skates, skate tours, skate patrol, a slalom course, clinics, hockey, speed skating, etc.

N.Y. State In-Line/Ice Skating Assn., Edwin Wagner, 518-885-6487, Ballston Spa, New York—Very family-oriented. Dual club: ice skate once or twice a week in winter, in-line twice a week in summer. Working on forming ten new clubs in the area. Has a waiting list of 80 people.

North Carolina

Charlotte Blade Rollers, Jack or Dailene Wilson, 704-344-1555, Charlotte, North Carolina—Club meets four times weekly. Beginners meet twice weekly. Produce bimonthly newsletter. Jack and Dailene are IISA-certified.

Tri-Ad In-Line Skate Club, Ryka Edwards, 910-945-4799, Lewisville, North Carolina—Meets Sunday afternoons for group skates. The club also participates in races.

Triangle Skating Club, Matt Cohen, 919-460-0964 or 919-783-0069, Research Triangle Park, North Carolina—Two weekend skates: Saturday at 10 a.m. and Sunday at 1 p.m.,in addition to Tuesday and Thursday skates. Geared toward intermediates, but beginners' clinics are available.

Ohio

Miami Valley In-Line Skaters Club, Tom Davis, 513-294-8817, Dayton, Ohio—Organizes group skates and races as well as skating clinics. Consists mainly of adults over 30.

Pennsylvania

Delaware Valley In-Line Skating Association (DVISA), Robert Gollwitzer, 215-236-7719, 2037 North Street, Philadelphia, Pennsylvania 19130—Organizes the Rollerjam demo series, provides other services and events.

Landskaters In-Line Skate Club, Doug Kelly, 609-854-7774 or 215-236-7119, Philadelphia, Pennsylvania—Weekly city skates: 8-mile tour of Philadelphia for experienced skaters. Monthly road trips to New York, Washington, New Jersey shore, etc. Weekly two-hour instructional clinics. Beginners welcome.

The Omni Speed Club and U.S.M.A.I.L., Buggy Allmond, 215-537-1692, Philadelphia, Pennsylvania—Indoor and outdoor speed-skating teams.

Pittsburgh In-Line Skate Club, Amy Krut, 412-885-2233, Pittsburgh, Pennsylvania—Thursday night skates through Oakland. South Side Bar Rolls: skate from bar to bar. Dinner Rolls: skate to a restaurant for dinner.

South Carolina

Grand Strand Beach Bladers, Charlie Belissary, 803-626-7245, Myrtle Beach, South Carolina—A casual group of 25–30 skaters who meet every Sunday at 3 P.M. for a group skate.

Texas

Interplanetary In-Line Skate Coalition, Darren Jenks, 806-371-3020, Amarillo, Texas.

Virginia

Beach Skater Club, Barbara Messner, 804-422-1902, Virginia Beach, Virginia—Puts on small skating events and other social events.

Washington

Acorn Club, Mike Flemming, 509-468-7866 or 509-466-1136, Mead, Washington—A new club that teaches beginner and intermediate skating and roller hockey.

Boeing Employees Blades on Pavement, Bruce Willard, 206-631-3047, Seattle, Washington—Monday night skates and whatever else evolves.

Team SK8 4 KIX, Penny Wagoner, 206-835-8485, Camas, Washington—A progressive, in-line skating team. Conducts public demonstrations, promotes lessons, and is led by a certified instructor.

Local Roller Hockey Clubs
Alabama

Hills Roller Hockey, Roland Markwalter, 205-883-9917, Huntsville, Alabama—4-on-4 plus goalkeeper. 32 teams, 60 adults and 60 kids.

Arizona

Hockey on Wheels, Dick Leopold, 602-267-7671, Phoenix, Arizona—4-on-4 plus goalkeeper. Three 13-week leagues for ages 9–13, 14–17, and 18+.

Southwestern Hockey Assn., Greg MacLellan, 602-968-5201, Tempe, Arizona—Has three in-line leagues: ages 9–11, 12–15, and 16+. Floor hockey for ages 16+. Open hockey: 6 p.m. Monday and Thursday for ages 16+, 5 p.m. Friday for ages 9–15.

California

Central Coast Roller Hockey League, Don Puett, 805-772-7851, Morro Bay, California—4-on-4 with goalkeeper. Freshman division, ages 6–9; sophomore, 10–13; junior, 14–16; and adult, 17+.

Central Coast Roller Hockey League, Rudy Zontini, 805-239-8650, Paso Robles, California—All ages from 7 to adult. Four women's teams. 250 players total.

Get InLine, 707-542-7914, Santa Rosa, California—Junior and women's leagues. Juniors meet twice a week during school; women's league meets once a week.

Golden West Hockey League, Kathy Shaw, 714-827-3480, Cypress, California—4-on-4. Tournament events twice a month. Practice and pickup hockey.

Gremic Roller Hockey, Mike Fisher, 408-971-2200, San Jose, California—4-on-4 plus goalkeeper. 10-week seasons. Three junior divisions, four adult divisions. Youth games on weekends, most adult games Sunday–Thursday, pickup games Friday.

InLine Sports, Tom Myers, 408-252-5233, San Jose, California—Three hockey rinks. Open to all types of leagues.

Recreation Division and Club Division, Neal Ryon, 310-425-7431, Lakewood, California—340 kids in rec division and 140 in club division, all under 16.

RHI Skate Center, Diane Thompson, 619-299-2460, San Diego, California—4-on-4. Continuous leagues throughout the year. 32 adult teams in three divisions, 20 youth teams in four divisions, one women's league.

San Juan Spurs, Diane Schneider, 714-493-5911, San Juan Capistrano, California— 150 players skate on Saturdays in fall, winter, and spring seasons. 200 players skate on weeknights during summer league. Registration is open until the leagues fill up. Players are placed into teams by age and ability.

Torrance Skate Assn., 310-320-9529, Torrance, California—5-on-5 for kids and lower adults, 4-on-4 for advanced. Four-month seasons.

Tri-Valley Roller Hockey League, Walter Collins or Debbie Chrisman, 805-373-6881, Thousand Oaks, California—5-on-5 plus goalkeeper. Spring and fall seasons. 10 games/season plus playoffs. Three age divisions: mite division, ages 7–9; midget, 10–12; and bantam, 13–15. Play with puck.

Florida

Acme Recreational Roller Hockey, Deborah Richards, 407-793-8600, Wellington, Florida— Training sessions for ages 5–7. Teams for ages 7–17. Practice once or twice a week. Play games once a week, year round, three seasons.

Astro Roller Hockey, Chris Maganias, 813-938-5778, Tarpon Springs, Florida—Hockey league skates Sunday, Monday, and Wednesday nights, and Saturday afternoons.

Atlantis League Hockey, Denise Savala or T. J. Mathieu, 407-837-2713, West Palm Beach, Florida—

Three youth leagues: peewee, ages 4–7; junior, 8–11; and senior, 12–16. Four adult leagues for ages 16 + : novice, players just learning to skate or play hockey; BB division, intermediate players; B division, advanced; and A division, more advanced, uses a puck. 200 adults, 200 kids. Considering expansion. Three seasons: August–December, January–May, May–August.

Conch Republic Roller Hockey, Joe Godbout, 305-743-8431, Marathon, Florida— Adult league for ages 18 + and two youth leagues: ages 8–12 and 12–18. Season runs November through April. Practice twice weekly, games on weekends. Adults play a 20-game schedule; youth play a 30-game schedule. One adult team and one youth all-star team travel to tournaments in off-season.

GOSCO Inc. (Grass Roots In-Line Hockey Tournaments & Promotions), Go Giannotta, 305-380-8866, Miami, Florida—Every year hosts one major tournament that caters to youths age 17 and under.

Hammock's Roller Hockey Club/Ryan's Roller Hockey Shop, Tom Ryan, 305-386-0037, Miami, Florida—Youth club, ages 7–17. Starting a club for ages 18 + .

Hot Wheels Roller Hockey League, Tom Mitchell, 305-255-4144, Miami, Florida—Youth league for ages 7 and under, 8–10, and 11–16. 12-week fall season beginning in September, 20-week winter season beginning in January. Also offers a learn-to-play-hockey program. Plans to offer a roller/ice hockey camp.

Jacksonville Hockey Assn., Bob Sabourin, 904-399-3223, Jacksonville, Florida—Summer and winter leagues. Midget division, ages 2–14; two junior divisions, 15–17; adult beginners, 18+; advanced division, 18+. Instructional clinics taught by professionals.

Panama City Roller Hockey Club, Jim Pigneri, 904-769-9415/Brian Street, 904-785-2261, Panama City, Florida—New club. Senior league, ages 17+. Junior league, ages 7–12 and 13–16. Both play year round and have travel teams.

Space Coast Roller Hockey Club, Mike Ferdinand, 407-259-7585, Melbourne, Florida—Coed youth and adult leagues. Seasons run September–December, January–April, and May–August. USAC-certified coaches. One indoor rink, two outdoors and building a third. Also offers clinics. Soon will offer ice hockey.

Stuart Sharks Roller Hockey Club, Kevin Carroll, 407-220-1488, Stuart, Florida—Five age divisions: 8 and under, 9–11, 12–14, 15–17, and 18+. Year-round, 10-week leagues. Pickup games for adults.

Sunshine Skate Equipment, Chris Hoag, 813-855-2154, Oldsmar, Florida—Sponsors various leagues in the area.

Tallahassee Roller Hockey Club, Steve Bohl, 904-656-2056, Tallahassee, Florida—Year-round club for ages 18+. Play twice weekly.

Totally Active Sports, Jon Novosielski, 813-367-7059, St. Petersburg, Florida—Contact for information on pickup games in the area.

Universal Skate Center, Tom Reeves, 407-282-3141, Orlando, Florida—Roller hockey league with about 258 players in four divisions: ages 10 and under, 11–13, 14–17, and 18+. Games Thursday, Saturday, and Sunday. Three seasons: summer, July–August; fall, October–December; and winter, February–May. Also offers artistic skating and speed-skating clubs.

West Kendall Roller Hockey Club, Bill Green, 305-386-2453, Miami, Florida—Coed leagues. Adult league for ages 18+, and three youth leagues: 9 and under, 12 and under, and 17 and under. 20 youth teams play Saturday morning. 12 adult teams play Sunday. Two seasons: mid-September through mid-December and January–May. Play outdoors.

Illinois

Chicago In-Line Hockey League, 312-665-0561, Chicago, Illinois.

Mt. Vernon Roller Hockey, 618-242-5712, Mt. Vernon, Illinois—4-on-4 with goalkeeper. Adult league. Eight teams with 150 members. Indoor fall league with two facilities.

Village Skate In-Line Hockey, John Pellettiere, 708-566-2590, Mundelein, Illinois—Men's and boys' leagues. Open practice Sunday morning.

Indiana

Indianapolis In-Line Skate Club, Matt Hart, 317-921-8810/574-CLUB, Indianapolis, Indiana—Primarily a skating club with its own hockey league.

Louisiana

Park Sk8 Inc., Wayne Aucoin, 504-891-7055, New Orleans, Louisiana—Junior leagues and clinics on Sunday. Adult leagues Sunday and Wednesday.

Massachusetts

Hudson Street Hockey, 508-562-3640, Hudson, Massachusetts.

Metro West In-Line Skate Club, Mark Caseau, 508-881-1322, Ashland, Massachusetts—Indoor, year-round facility. Offers adult and youth coed street and roller hockey leagues and tournaments. Public skate hours. Special hours/lessons available for club members, beginning through advanced.

New England In-Line Hockey League, Tim O'Connell, 617-269-0087, Boston, Massachusetts—24 teams in a league with 225 participants.

South Shore Sports Center, Ted, 617-740-1105, Hingham, Massachusetts—Youth league forming to play on indoor street-hockey rink.

Michigan

Detroit Roller Hockey Assn., Ken, 810-558-9211; Chris, 810-731-7191; Kevin, 810-852-8291, Warren, Michigan—Has approximately 800 members, ages 8–45. Leagues break down into the following age groups: 8 and under; 9–12; 13–17; and 18+. Also has the USAC/RS Gold Division team.

Missouri

Florissant Roller Hockey, Ron Beilsten, 314-839-0515, Florissant, Missouri—League consists of 35 teams, about 400 kids ages 5–16. Kids play in a round-robin within their age groups: 9 and under, 10–11, 12–13, and 14–16.

Kansas City Roller Hockey Assn., John Grandbouche, 816-741-1281, Kansas City, Missouri—Has one league that plays in three rinks: Trenton, Missouri; Liberty, Missouri; and Kansas City, Kansas. 242 players. No fees. 90 percent in-line skaters. Trying to find funding for an outdoor facility so membership can increase.

New Jersey

New Jersey Rock & Rollers, Moriko Nishiura, 201-538-6012, Cedar Knolls, New Jersey—Offers youth, teen, and adult leagues, and in-line clinics.

Rip Blade Hockey of Jersey City, Tom Kaz, 201-659-7516, Jersey City, New Jersey—4-on-4. Eight teams, 110 members. Spring, summer, and fall seasons. Ages 15–35. Rink slightly smaller than regulation size. Use ball.

Tansboro In-Line/Dekhockey League (DVISA), Ray deRosa, 609-768-3044, Tansboro, New Jersey— Roller hockey league on full-size rink with Sport Court surface, boards, lights, and electronic scoreboard.

New Mexico

New Mexico Roller Hockey, Bud Witte, 505-298-9889, Albuquerque, New Mexico— Four divisions: junior, 12 and under; teen, 13–17; adult, 13 + ; recreational, new players unfamiliar with roller hockey.

New York

American Hockey Center, Shelly or Ken Broman, 516-928-8901, Miller Place, New York— Approximately 40 teams consisting of a Penguin league for ages 6–10, a Beaver league for ages 10–13, a Cadet league for ages 13–16, a Freshman league for ages 16–19 (soon to be incorporated into the senior league), and Senior A & B leagues.

Bear Mountain Roller Hockey, Ron Schnell, 914-255-7231, New Paltz, New York—Has a youth instructional program and adult hockey league. Each team plays twice a week outdoors at Bear Mountain State Park. In its sixth season. 200 adults, 100 kids. Uses a puck. No checking. Sanctioned by NIHA.

Liverpool Sports Center, John Chen, 315-457-2290, Liverpool, New York—In the process of developing a league in the Syracuse area. Currently planning to set up a lighted rink in a nearby park. Will charge for referees.

New York Roller Hockey League, Mike Bologna, 212-858-6386 (day) /718-626-6175 (night), New Paltz, New York—NIHA League. 5-on-5. Quad and in-line skates. No checking. New facility. 15 teams for first season. Putting together youth program. Season from May to September.

Queens Roller Hockey Assn., 718-275-0970, Kew Gardens, New York.

Valley Stream Roller Hockey, Marty Zirpolo/James Gaglione, 516-825-8570/791-9609, Valley Stream, New York—Instructional clinic, 4 and under; squirt division, 5–6; peewee division, 7–9; midget A and B divisions, 10–12; intermediate division, 13–14; junior division, 15–16; adult A and B divisions, 17 + ; masters division, 35 + .

Oklahoma

Tulsa Hockey Sales, Carry Eskrige, 918-252-0729/832-0118, Tulsa, Oklahoma—10-week, year-round roller hockey leagues. Ages: 7 and under, 9 and under, 12 and under, 15 and under, 17 and under, and 18+. One game and one practice per week.

Pennsylvania

Central Penn Roller Hockey, Scott Matincheck, 717-944-7866, Middletown, Pennsylvania—Usually two traveling teams consisting of 12 players each. Teams practice year round. Planning a Thursday night league.

Texas

Holiday Roller Rink, 817-838-5738, Ft. Worth, Texas—Youth roller hockey.

Wheels in Motion, Lea Crowe, 214-644-2221, Richardson, Texas—Mainly a roller hockey club. The team teaches the basics, and pickup games are played each Tuesday.

Washington

Mercer Island Roller Hockey League, Jeff Carroll, 206-232-7806, Mercer Island, Washington—This is a new youth roller hockey league forming just outside of Seattle.

British Columbia

Whistler Wheels In-Line Skate Club, Simon Hudson, 604-932-7201, Whistler, British Columbia, Canada—Four levels. Two levels offer instruction on roller hockey by certified hockey coaches. Holds hockey tournaments.

APPENDIX B

IN-LINE MEDIA

PERIODICALS

American Hockey Magazine, 4965 North 30th Street, Colorado Springs, CO 80919. 800-521-8381. Published eight times annually. Covers in-line and ice hockey. Subscriptions are $25 per year (U.S.), $29 per year (foreign).

InLine magazine, 2025 Pearl Street, Boulder, CO 80302. 303-440-5111; 800-877-5281. Published six times annually. Subscriptions are $29.97 per year. This glossy, full-color, large-format magazine is fun to read or breeze through. Stories may be instructional or reflective;

interviews are also included. Covers most major aspects of the sport.

Skater's Edge, Box 500, Kensington, MD 20895. 301-946-1971. Subscriptions are $15 per year in the U.S., $20/U.S. in Canada. This is a newsletter about ice, in-line, and roller skating published five times per year.

Speedskating Times, 2910 Northeast 11th Avenue., Pompano Beach, FL 33064. 305-782-5928. A tabloid newspaper published eight times year. Covers ice speed skating and in-line speed skating. Keeps track of events and racing skates, technique.

U.S. Rollerskating, 4730 South Street, P.O. Box 6579, Lincoln, NE 68506-0579. Published monthly (except August) by the U.S. Amateur Confederation of Roller Skating. Subscriptions are $10 per year (U.S.), $15 per year (foreign).

MOVIES AND VIDEOS

Airborne, 1993. 1 hour, 30 minutes. Distributed by Warner Brothers. (PG) Starring Shane McDermott, Seth Green and Brittney Powell. Summary: Teenage California in-line skater and surfer Mitchell Goosen (Shane McDermott) is forced to move to Cincinnati. There, ice and roller hockey are big sports. Mitchell irritates some students, but shows through his prowess, Zen qualities, and pacifism that he's a good guy.

Rollerblade Ready Set . . . Roll! In-line skating as taught by top instructors. A 15-minute video on the basics. Topics covered include fit, protective equipment, ready position, stopping, turning, striding, and rules of the road. Features Jill Schulz and Chris Mitchell, Team Rollerblade members; Eric Flaim, Olympic ice speed skating/Rollerblade Racing Team member; Kalinda Aaron, IISA examiner. Directed by Ken Greer. Produced by Freer & Associates. For further information, call Rollerblade Inc. at 800-232-ROLL.

Scott Cramer's How to In-Line Skate: BASIC Skills ($19.95; 23 minutes). This tape provides an introduction to in-line skating, including protective gear, starting and stopping, the stride, turning, crossovers, backward skating, and more, with instruction by U.S. and world professional ice skating champion Scott Cramer. (To order any of Scott Cramer's tapes, send a check or money order to: BLB Products, P.O. Box 38485, Colorado Springs, CO 80937, 800-833-9294. Allow 3–4 weeks for delivery.)

Scott Cramer's How To In-Line Skate: ADVANCED Skills ($19.95; 28 minutes). Cramer continues instructing, this time focusing on transitions, one-foot turns, control moves, tricks, spinning, advanced stopping and more.

Scott Cramer's In-Line Skating Dances ($29.95; 90 minutes). Here, Cramer covers 16 in-line dances, beginning with easy and progressing to difficult dances. Includes both solo and with-a-partner type dances. Intended for skaters who have progressed beyond his first videos, those who are intrigued by learning in-line dance, and those who just want to witness the beauty of in-line dance.

Skate to Ski, produced by Rollerblade Inc. with the Professional Ski Instructors of America and the United Skates Ski Team. For further information, call Rollerblade Inc. at 800-232-ROLL.

APPENDIX C

MANUFACTURERS AND VENDORS

SKATES

Atomic Ski USA Inc., 9 Columbia Dr., Amherst, NH 03031-2306. Tel: 603-880-6143; 800-258-5020. Fax: 603-626-4833.

Austin Sportsgear Inc. (ASI), 621 Liberty St., Jackson, MI 49203. Tel: 517-784-1120. Fax: 517-784-5085.

Bauer/Canstar. Tel: 800-622-2189; 802-868-2711.

Brookfield Athletic Co. Inc., 13 Centennial Dr., Peabody, MA 01960-7901. Tel: 508-532-9000; 800-477-6553. Fax: 508-532-6105.

California Pro Inc., 8102 White Horse Rd., Greenville, SC 29611-1836. Tel: 803-294-5370; 800-932-5777. Fax: 803-294-5236.

Canstar Sports USA Inc./Bauer, P.O. Box 716, 50 Jonergin Dr., Swanton, VT 05488-0716. Tel: 802-868-2711; 800-622-2189. Fax: 802-868-3789.

CCM/Sports Maska, 7405 Trans Canada Highway, Suite 300, St. Lauerent, Quebec, Canada H4Y1Z2. Tel: 514-331-5150. Fax: 514-331-7061.

Concept Design, Palo Alto, CA. Tel: 415-493-1117.

Exel Marketing (Roces), 1 Second Street, Peabody, MA 01960. Tel: 508-532-2226. Fax: 508-532-3728.

First Team Sports Inc., 2274 Woodale Dr., Mounds View, MN 55112-4900. Tel: 612-780-4454; 800-458-2250. Fax: 612-780-8908.

K2 Corporation, 19215 Vashon Highway S.W., Vashon, WA 98070-5236. Tel: 206-463-3631; 800-426-1617. Fax: 206-463-5463.

Karhu U.S.A., 55 Green Mountain Drive, P.O. Box 4249, South Burlington, VT 05406. Tel: 802-864-4519. Fax: 802-864-6774.

Kazaz Inc., P.O. Box 23445, Richfield, MN 55423-0445. Tel: 612-224-5700; 800-257-3550. Makers of Koho, Jofa, Titan, and Canadian brands of equipment.

Lake Placid Figure Skates, P.O. Box 930, Litchfield, IL 62056-0930. Tel: 217-324-3961. Fax: 217-324-2213.

Maska. *See* CCM/Sports Maska.

National Sporting Goods, 25 Brighton Ave, Passaic, NJ 07055-2001. Tel: 201-779-2323; 800-242-7476. Fax: 201-779-0084.

Oberhamer Inc., 11975 Portland Ave S, Ste. 122, Burnsville, MN 55337-1530. Tel: 612-890-1657. Fax: 612-890-0511.

Oxygen Skates. *See* Atomic Ski USA.

Riedell Shoes Inc., P.O. Box 21, Red Wing, MN 55066-0021. Tel: 612-388-8251. Fax: 612-388-8616.

Roce. *See* Exel Marketing.

Roller Derby Skate Corp., 311 W Edwards St., Litchfield, IL 62056-1904. Tel: 217-324-3961. Fax: 217-324-2213.

Rollerblade, Inc., 5101 Shady Oak Rd., Minnetonka, MN 55343-4314. Tel: 612-930-7000; 800-232-ROLL. Fax: 612-930-7040.

Seneca Sports Inc., P.O. Box 719, Milford, MA 01757-0719. Tel: 508-634-3616. Fax: 508-634-8154.

Ultra Wheels, 2274 Woodale Drive, Mounds View, MN 55112. Tel: 612-780-4454; 800-458-2250. Fax: 612-780-8908.

Variflex, 5152 N. Commerce Ave., Moorpark, CA 93021. Tel: 805-523-0322.

Zepter Sports Int'l, 12780 High Bluff Dr., Ste. 200, San Diego, CA 92130. Tel: 619-530-0844.

WHEELS

Core Speedwheels. 2554 Lincoln Boulevard, Suite 244, Venice, CA 90291. Tel: 800-987-4450. Fax: 310-574-8108. E-mail: COREshls@ix.netcom.com.

The Hyper Corporation, 15241 Transistor, Huntington Beach, CA 92649. Tel: 714-373-3300. Fax: 714-373-2525.

Kryptonics Inc., 740 South Pierce, Louisville, CO 80027. Tel: 303-665-5353. Fax: 303-665-1318.

Labeda. 18650 Collier Avenue, Unit A, Lake Elsinore, CA 92530. Tel: 909-674-1665. Fax: 909-674-2518.

Roller Edge In-Line Skate Wheels, 16 Western Industrial Drive, Cranston, RI 02921-3405. Tel: 800-757-3343. Fax: 401-943-8210.

Roller Edge Live Actions Wheels. 800-757-EDGE. Hockey-oriented wheels.

BEARINGS

Black Hole Performance, P.O. Box 20, Mercer Island, WA 98040. Tel: 206-236-4500; 800-327-9393. Fax: 206-236-5490.

Bones Swiss Bearings, Powell Corporation, 30 S. La Patera Lane, Santa Barbara, CA 93117. Tel: 800-288-7528.

Boss Swiss Bearings., Hyperwheels, 15241 Transistor Lane, Huntington Beach, CA 92649. Tel: 800-BE-HYPER.

Twin-Cam/Asia Access Inc., 1123 Riverwood Drive, Burnsville, MN 55337. Tel: 612-890-6368; 800-382-2793. Fax: 612-890-6388.

PROTECTIVE GEAR

Aggro Sports, 2125 San Joaquin Hills Road, Newport Beach, CA 92660. Tel: 714-644-9477; 800-644-9477. Fax: 714-644-7500. Makes Aggro sport Hip Checks. These are padded hip and rear protectors, with skid plates. $49.95 + shipping and handling.

Andiamo. Tel: 208-726-1385.

Aria Sonics. Tel: 800-682-2724. After you push a button, the Aria Sonics helmet inflates to best fit your head.

Austin SportsGear. Tel: 517-784-1120. Hip protection.

Bauer. Tel: 800-362-3146. Helmet-knee-elbow-wrist protection.

Bell Sport Inc., Route 136 East, Rantoul, IL 61866. Tel: 217-893-9300. Fax: 217-892-8727. Helmets.

Boneless. Tel: 801-627-3292. Knee-elbow-wrist.

CCM/Sports Maska, 7405 Trans Canada Highway, Suite 300, St. Lauerent, Quebec Canada H4Y1Z2. Tel: 514-331-5150. Fax: 514-331-7061. Helmets.

CDS Detroit. Tel: 313-331-7371. Gloves.

Crash Pads. Tel: 800-964-5993 Hip-leg-tailbone protection.

Great State Hockey Supply Company, 3395 Sheridan Drive, Amherst, NY 14226. Tel: 800-828-7496. Fax: 716-838-5123. This company offers a highly detailed seventy-page, free, catalog of hockey-related gear, including protective equipment.

Lazzy Legs. Tel: 909-695-6883. Knee-elbow-wrist protection.

Louis Garneau USA, 66 Main St., Box 755, Newport, VT 05855-2121. Tel: 802-334-5885; 800-448-1984. Fax: 802-334-6425. Helmets.

LT. Tel: 719-637-0010. Helmets.

Oxygen. Tel: 800-258-5020. Helmet-knee-elbow-wrist.

Pro Designed. Tel: 713-957-0341. Knee-elbow-tailbone.

Pro-Tec. Tel: 206-872-3300. Helmet maker-makes specialty helmets for vert skaters.

Rector. 586 Martin Avenue, No. 6, Rohnert Park, CA 94928. Tel: 707-544-5044; 800-248-5633. Protective gear.

Roces. Tel: 800-343-5200. Knee-elbow-wrist.

Rollerblade Inc., 5101 Shady Oak Rd. Minnetonka, MN 55343. Tel: 612-930-7000. Fax: 612-930-7030. Helmet-knee-elbow-wrist.

Seirus. Tel: 800-447-3787. Knee-elbow-wrist.

Seneca Sports Inc. Tel: 506-634-3616. Knee-elbow-wrist.

Thunderwear, Tel: 714-492-1141. Knee-elbow-wrist.

Troxel, Tel: 619-429-1441. Protective gear.

Ultra Wheels, 2274 Woodale Drive, Mounds View, MN 55112. Tel: 612-780-4454. Fax: 612-780-9327. Helmet-knee-elbow-wrist.

Wayley Shorts, Tel: 303-494-8255. Heavy-duty shorts with removable hip and tailbone pads.

World Sports Int'l, Tel: 508-867-4411. Knee-elbow-wrist.

HOCKEY GEAR

CCM/Sports Maska, 7405 Trans Canada Highway, Suite 300, St. Lauerent, Quebec Canada H4Y1Z2. Tel: 514-331-5150. Fax: 514-331-7061. Chest-shoulders-gloves-elbow-knee-stick.

GDS Sports. Tel: 800-800-7120. Makers of the Shooter Tutor goal-shooting system.

Great Skate Hockey Supply Company, 3395 Sheridan Drive, Amherst, NY 14226. Tel: 716-838-5123. Fax 716-838-5100. Provides an excellent free catalog.

Hot Pucks. 800-933-PUCK. Fax: 612-935-9142.

In-Line Sport Systems Inc., 821 Marquette Ave., Suite 2300, Minneapolis, MN 55402. Tel: 612-342-2337. Fax: 612-338-2302. This company makes a system of 50 foam pads that, when set-up, make a border for a rink. For further information or a brochure call 800-809-RINK.

JOFA and KOHO—See Karhu, p. 214.

Tour Hockey Skates. P.O. Box 930, Litchfield, IL 62056. Tel: 217-324-3961. Fax: 217-324-2213.

ACCESSORIES AND MISCELLANEOUS

Andiamo!, Box 1657, Sun Valley, ID 83353-1657. Tel: 208-726-1385. Fax: 208-726-1388.

Aria Sonics Inc., 3678 Mount Diablo Blvd., Ste. A, Lafayette, CA 94549-3715. Tel: 510-284-3752; 800-682-2742. Fax: 510-284-3753.

Austin Sportsgear Inc. (ASI), 621 Liberty St., Jackson, MI 49203. Tel: 517-784-1120. Fax: 517-784-5085.

Black Hole Performance, P.O. Box 20, Mercer Island, WA 98040. Tel: 206-236-4500; 800-327-9393.

Boca Bearing Co., 7040 W Palmetto Park Rd., Ste. 2304-S, Boca Raton, FL 33433. Tel: 800-332-3256.

Body Armor Inc., 4900 Prospectus Dr., Ste. 200, Durham, NC 27713. Tel: 919-544-8711.

Chisco Sport Accessories, 2550 South 2300 West, Ste. 1, Salt Lake City, UT 84119-2052. Tel: 801-972-5656; 800-825-4555. Fax: 801-972-5690.

Commit Enterprises. Tel: 310-576-0033. Grind Plates.

Etto Helmets, 888 Research Dr., #105, Palm Springs, CA 92262-5938. Tel: 619-778-1242; 800-452-5819. Fax: 619-778-1245.

GRIP In-Line Speed Control, GRIP Inc., 5375 Western Avenue, Suite D-1, Boulder, CO 80301. Tel: 800-510-GRIP. Grip makes a system of hand-controlled brakes that attach to special wheels provided. See detailed description in Chapter 3.

Hickory Industries, 429 27th St., NW, Hickory, NC 28601-4549. Tel: 704-322-2600; 800-438-5777. Fax: 704-328-1700.

Hyper Inline Corp., 15241 Transistor Lane, Huntington Beach, CA 92649-1141. Tel: 714-373-3300; 800-234-9737. Fax: 714-373-2525.

Innovative Sport Systems Inc., 7680 Golden Triangle Dr., Eden Prairie, MN 55344-3732. Tel: 612-941-1916; 800-321-7948. Fax: 612-941-8944.

Itech Sports Products, U.S.A. Inc.

Kryptonics Inc., 7405 Pierce Ave., S, Louisville, CO 80027-3023. Tel: 303-665-5353; 800-766-9146. Fax: 303-665-1318.

Lazzy Legs, 43089 Business Park Dr., Temecula, CA 92590. Tel: 800-821-1785.

Mackay Int'l Inc., 5041 W Knoll Dr., Yorba Linda, CA 92686. Tel: 714-777-9069.

Mulholland Development Company, Tel: 415-455-0700. Reflective gear.

NDL Products Inc., 2313 NW 30th Pl., Pompano Beach, FL 33069-0701. Tel: 305-942-4560; 800-843-3021. Fax: 305-978-9496.

Nucom/Grizzly, 5612 International Pkwy., New Hope, MN 55337. Tel: 612-535-2035.

Out of Line Sports, Inc. 3140 South Williams, Englewood, CO 80110. Makes heel brake mechanism for retro-fitting.

Paragon, Tel: 800-328-4827, ext. 4656; or 612-442-6364. Reflective gear.

Reflex, Tel: 800-552-6064. Reflective gear.

Roller Guard, Tel: 800-667-8103. Roller Guards are plastic guards that cover the wheels and provide a flat surface for walking. They are strapped to the tops of your boots.

Santa Cruz Snowboards Inc., 104 Bronson St., Santa Cruz, CA 95062-3489. Tel: 408-459-7800; 800-543-7979. Fax: 408-459-7820.

Sun Hockey Inc., P.O. Box 36155 Pentagon Towers, Edina, MN 55435-6155. Tel: 800-933-7825; 800-933-7825. Fax: 612-935-9142.

Thunderwear Inc., 1060-C Calle Negocio, San Clemente, CA 92673-6205. Tel: 714-492-1141; 800-422-6565. Fax: 714-492-3259.

Twincam/Asia Access Inc., 1123 Riverwood Dr., Burnsville, MN 55337. Tel: 800-382-2793.

Valeo Inc., W229N1680 Westwood Dr., Waukesha, WI 53186-1152. Tel: 414-547-9474; 800-634-2704. Fax: 414-547-5270.

Yak Research, 850 W MacArthur Blvd., Oakland, CA 94608. Tel: 800-488-9257.

VistaLite, Tel: 800-776-5677. Reflective gear.

Windskate, Inc., P.O. Box 3081, Santa Monica, CA 90403. Tel: 303-453-4808. Produces a hand-held sail for skaters.

APPENDIX D

ANNUAL EVENTS

Athens to Atlanta RoadRunners Marathon.

This 85-mile event is skated every October and is organized by the Atlanta Peachtree Roadrollers. For information, write: Atlanta Peachtree Roadrollers, P.O. Box 15482, Atlanta, GA 30333, or call 404-634-9032.

National In-Line Skate Series.

This is a tour of professional skaters in many categories. Contact Rick Stark of Anywhere Sports Producitons. Tel: 310-826 5464. Fax: 310-447-5906.

New York Road Skaters Marathon.

This is an annual competition. Steve Novack or Priscilla Bohm are organizers. They may be reached at 212-534-7858.

Triple Crown/Bauer Roller Hockey Challenge.

This is a touring playoff competion and demo that is open to amatuer roller hockey participants. Will hit 45 cities in 1995. Features a radar slap shot contest, skill competitions, playoffs, and other events. Contact: David King. Tel: 303-224-2502.

INDEX